MAKING THE STUDENT TEACHING:

Successful Student Teaching for the Aspiring Educator

Michelle Kurchian, M. Ed.
Catherine Giles, M. Ed.

Fourth Edition (2014)
Copyright 2008
ISBN 978-1-312-85449-9

DEDICATION

We dedicate this handbook to all of the student teachers with whom we have had the opportunity and pleasure to learn and grow over the years. Thank you for your dedication, hard work, and efforts that went "above and beyond." We are proud to say that you were once our student teachers and hope that someday you will become cooperating teachers for other aspiring educators.

MK and CG

ABOUT THE AUTHORS

Ms. MICHELLE KURCHIAN has been an elementary- and middle school-certified educator for over fifteen years. During this time, Ms. Kurchian has served as a fifth grade self-contained, inclusion, and specialty math teacher, as a library media specialist, as a graduate professor of literacy courses, and as a cooperating practitioner to many undergraduate and graduate students. In addition, she has also served in the role of mentor to newly hired teachers in the Reading Public Schools and as a supervisor of high school students planning to enter the field of education. Ms. Kurchian is honored to be considered a role model and partner to aspiring and new teachers and plans to continue in this capacity as she feels it is an extremely worthwhile and rewarding experience.

Mrs. CATHERINE GILES has been certified as an early childhood/inclusion model teacher for the past nineteen years, during which time she has served as cooperating practitioner to numerous undergraduate and graduate student teachers. She has also been an on-site supervisor to student teachers from local colleges. After earning a National Certification in Early Childhood Education, Mrs. Giles became a Department of Education certified mentor teacher and has formally mentored a number of newly hired teachers in the Reading Public Schools in Reading, MA. Most recently, Mrs. Giles was honored with the recognition of being named a Mentor Teacher of the Year through the Massachusetts Association of Curriculum and Development. Mrs. Giles is passionate about supervising and mentoring new and aspiring teachers. Now an elementary school principal, Mrs. Giles plans to continue fostering positive student teacher-cooperating teacher relationships within her own school. In doing so, she believes that the possibilities are endless for everyone involved!

Together, Ms. Kurchian and Mrs. Giles have also written a guide for parents on reading with their children.

Fourth Edition 2014
Copyright 2008
Michelle Kurchian and Catherine Giles
ISBN 978-1-312-85449-9

MAKING THE MOST OF STUDENT TEACHING:
Successful Student Teaching for the Aspiring Educator

Aspiring Educator,

     Congratulations and welcome to your student teaching! This handbook will help you prepare for and guide you through one of the most memorable experiences of your educational journey. Thanks to dedicated and knowledgeable instructors, you have acquired a solid foundation of professional and academic content background upon which to build with an experience-based practicum.

     The underlying goal of this practicum guide is to provide everyone involved, including the youngest of students, a successful learning experience. Therefore, in addition to guiding the student teacher through a successful practicum, the roles of the cooperating practitioner, and to some extent the supervisor, have been kept in mind as well.

Cooperating Practitioner,

     Congratulations! As cooperating practitioner, you will serve as the primary influence and role model for an eager, aspiring educator. You are encouraged to share your expertise, resources, and time as you guide and direct, essentially shape, a new teacher.

A Supervisory Note

Details of the supervisor's role may vary from college to college and state to state. However, the supervisor will always be a key player in a successful student teaching experience. He/she will serve as a central communicator and coordinator of the entire placement experience. The supervisor will assist in important record-keeping and give invaluable feedback about the student teacher's current performance. He/she is on your side! Staying "on the same page" with your college supervisor will pave the way for a smooth student teaching experience.

MAKING THE MOST OF STUDENT TEACHING:
Successful Student Teaching
for the Aspiring Educator

YOU ONLY GET ONE CHANCE:
MAKING A POSITIVE FIRST IMPRESSION ON YOUR
COOPERATING PRACTITIONER

ON YOUR MARK, GET SET, GO: SETTING UP THE FIRST MEETING

First impressions are formed within 30 seconds or less, and since you only get one chance to make a first impression, get it right the first time!

If you receive your fall student teaching assignment in the spring, take advantage of an early start and call the assigned school. If you receive your assignment later, make this call prior to the start of the school year. If you will be completing your student teaching in the spring, for the second half of the year, be sure to make your initial contact as soon as you receive your placement. During this call, introduce yourself to the principal of the building, and ask if you may visit the school and meet your cooperating practitioner.

Try to set up a time that is convenient for your cooperating practitioner. Be sure check directions in advance (using Mapquest, Google, GPS), and give yourself plenty of time to be punctual. Park in an appropriate space, and enter the school through the main entrance. Report to the main office, politely introduce yourself, and explain the reason for your visit. If the principal happens to be available, introduce yourself to him or her as well.

BONUS POINTS

Research the school/district in advance by visiting its website and reading about its: mission statement, principal(s) and staff, curriculum, community, and technology availability.   This will give you a general idea of what type of experience to expect from your student teaching. In addition, you will appear prepared and informed when you ask relevant questions.

DRESS FOR SUCCESS: PREPARING FOR THE FIRST MEETING

Since 90% of a first impression is based on appearance and how you greet a person, pay close attention to these details and put your best foot forward!

APPEARANCE

At your first meeting and throughout your student teaching, you want your appearance to communicate respect and confidence. As a future teacher, dress accordingly: neatly and professionally. Your clothing does not need to be expensive to meet these requirements.

GREETING

How you greet future colleagues is equally as important as your attire. Your greeting should convey genuine feelings of excitement and enthusiasm for the adventure that lies ahead. Consider your posture, facial expression/body language, and tone of voice as you introduce yourself.

- POSTURE: Make the first move. Stand up straight and look each person in the eye as you offer a firm handshake.

- FACIAL EXPRESSION/BODY LANGUAGE: A smile is your best accessory when you meet someone new. Let your enthusiasm show, and communicate openness with a genuine smile and professional, yet relaxed body language.

- TONE OF VOICE: Think and be positive! A confident and friendly voice and manner set the tone for a successful new relationship.

TAKE NOTE: AGENDA FOR THE FIRST MEETING

Whether this meeting occurs in the spring, summer, or at the start of the school year, have a positive attitude and be prepared in order to get your student teaching experience off and running in the right direction.

Most likely, your cooperating practitioner will have an agenda for this first meeting. Since the goal of an initial meeting is to create a partnership with your cooperating practitioner, come prepared with an open mind (and an open notebook!) as well as any initial questions you may have. The following is a general guideline for helping your first meeting go smoothly.

INTRODUCTIONS

Introductions and pleasant, informal conversation will help you get personally acquainted. You may also be introduced to grade-level or other colleagues at this time. Your cooperating practitioner will most likely share his/her professional background and educational philosophy. You should share your educational background and experience as well as what inspired you to become a teacher. This adds to the first impression you make and gives a "snapshot" of who you are as an aspiring educator.

EXPECTATIONS, GENERAL RESPONSIBILITES, AND GOALS

Both you and your cooperating practitioner should be upfront and honest about your expectations for a successful semester. At this initial meeting, general responsibilities may be discussed. Be prepared to share your goals, too. What would you like to get out of this opportunity? (Remember, the goal at this early meeting is to set your mind at ease, not to overwhelm you. So don't overwhelm yourself! Keep the conversation general and worry-free. There will be plenty of time for details later.)

GET A HEAD START
At this time you may receive a "head start packet," a collection of information that can help you prepare for your practicum. It may include a general description of the district/school, mission statement, and/or general curriculum overviews. If not, just ask, "What can I do to prepare in advance?"

COLLEGE REQUIREMENTS
If you have a handbook from your college, share it with your cooperating practitioner at this time. If not, be sure to share it early in your practicum. Your cooperating practitioner wants to be just as prepared as you do!

CLOSURE
Remember, your cooperating practitioner is there to serve as your coach and to offer you support and encouragement. So be sure to share any thoughts and/or concerns you may have about your upcoming practicum. You may offer to exchange contact information. Also ask about your next meeting. If it is an option for you, offer to help set up the classroom before school begins. This can be a valuable bonding and learning experience. Otherwise, make sure you ask for important details about your first day: how to dress, what time to arrive, what to bring, where to park, etc.

The perfect ending to your first meeting is a brief tour/orientation of the classroom and school you'll be working in for the semester. If one isn't offered, just ask! Your early enthusiasm and initiative will pay off with one of the most rewarding experiences of your career in education.

NOW WHAT DO I DO?:
TAKING A CLOSER LOOK AT WEEK-BY-WEEK EXPECTATIONS

Expectations for student teaching will vary from classroom to classroom, grade level to grade level, school to school, and district to district. The following should serve as a general guideline as to what to expect during your student teaching.

BEFORE SCHOOL STARTS

Inquire if your cooperating practitioner would like any assistance setting up the classroom in advance. He/she may appreciate an extra pair of hands during this busy time. It can also give you a chance to get to know each other before the students arrive, as well as get acquainted with the classroom, general curriculum, and/or materials you could read in advance.

Coming in early may also open the door to opportunity. For example, perusing quality, education online resources about "back-to-school" activities may spark some ideas for you. Perhaps you could ask permission to design a welcome back bulletin board display. You might even offer to do a brief getting-to-know-you activity with the students early on. Showing ambition and initiative will let it be known that you are appreciative of your cooperating practitioner's willingness to open his/her classroom and demonstrate your eagerness to help out and become an active participant.

> NOTE: If you are an early childhood or middle school major, you will have to split your time between two classrooms, which means that the following guidelines could be accelerated. Although it may be more difficult the first time around, think of how prepared you'll be for round two!

Notice the **TAKE NOTE!** topics for the different weeks. These sections have been included to highlight important teaching tips, strategies, and practices. In addition, these are often the same topics about which interview questions are generated. Therefore, student teachers benefit from reflecting upon these **TAKE NOTE!** topics. If you spend time reflecting upon these topics weekly, by the end of your practicum, you will be well-prepared to answer many of your interview questions!

WEEKS 1-2: OFF ON THE RIGHT FOOT

FIRST DAY JITTERS
Even experienced teachers still get those butterflies! Get a good night's sleep, and eat a light, healthy breakfast. Pack a healthy snack and lunch as well. (Teachers need to keep their energy up!) Dress appropriately and wear a great big smile. Look at this day as the

very first day of an extremely rewarding career.

- Get to know the children – names and faces
  The children come first! Remember that you are their teacher above their friend and you will earn the students' respect right away.

- Familiarize yourself with the classroom
  Pay attention to the "traffic flow" and physical arrangement of the desks in the classroom. Also note how activity centers, literature displays, and curriculum materials are organized.

- Take a tour of the school
  Learn where the main office, art room, gym, cafeteria, staff room, media center/computer lab and library are located in relation to your classroom. Don't forget the restrooms!

- "Shadow" your cooperating practitioner
  Observe your cooperating practitioner's interactions with children, parents, and colleagues. When appropriate throughout student teaching, attend meetings with grade-level teams, parents, staff, curriculum committees, etc. Treat everyone with respect! You can learn a lot not only from your cooperating practitioner, but from his/her colleagues as well, particularly if you are genuinely interested in learning from their experience.

- Review college guidelines and/or handbook
  Stay in close contact with your college supervisor. Know when to schedule observations and when any assignments may be due. Also know in advance what you may need to accomplish for state certification.

- Observe daily attendance, homework, and dismissal routines
  Many times these routines are the first responsibilities of the student teacher. Pay close attention!

- Observe and assist students in all curriculum areas throughout the day
  This is your learning experience . . . ACTIVELY PARTICIPATE. To observe, circulate, assist students, take notes . . . don't just sit at the back of the room! Rule of thumb: If your cooperating teacher is not sitting, neither should you be!

- Begin to keep a weekly plan book
  Use your cooperating practitioner's plan book as a model. It may be an actual book or an online version. Later you can highlight lessons for which you are responsible.

- Introduce yourself to the families

    This will be the first impression you make upon parents. Use the same mode of communication currently used by your cooperating practitioner. (paper letter, email, blogs/wikis, etc.) Briefly introduce yourself, share your educational background, and stress your enthusiasm and appreciation that you will be a part of their children's education. After all, you will learn as much from them as they do from you! (Don't forget to have someone proofread your work – it is a reflection of you both personally and professionally!) An additional tip is to include with this letter a note asking for parent permission to take photos throughout your student teaching.

- Say "cheese"

    Start taking photos and video clips now. Be sure to include all the things you've personally created. And once you have parent permission, include students actively learning. These capture special memories as well as make a great addition to your professional portfolio (no names included, of course).

- Formulate questions to discuss with your cooperating teacher

    All questions are good questions! This is true throughout your student teaching, so keep asking! Also, find out your cooperating teacher's schedule. Is he/she an "early riser" or a "late-stayer"? It may be helpful to stick to a similar schedule. Setting up a regular meeting time convenient to both of you will prove extremely valuable since the school day can get so busy.

- Review school/district resource materials

    These resources, whether provided by your cooperating practitioner or available on the school's website, will provide you with background information that you can read on your own time. (If you can't locate this information, ask for it.)
    - School/district handbook
    - Curriculum rationale/overviews
    - Daily schedule including specialists
    - Map of school
    - School calendar
    - Fire drill or other emergency procedures
    - Class list
    - Discipline policy
    - Sample of progress report/report card
    - Medical information/training
    - District acceptable use policy

TAKE NOTE!

As you get more familiar with the routines of the classroom, begin to focus your attention more on *classroom management*.
- Transitions
- Discipline in specific situations
- Attention-getting techniques
- Monitoring of students during and between lessons
- Positive reinforcement
- Consequences

WEEK 3: GETTING YOUR FEET WET
In addition to the above,

- Greet each child or any parent upon entering the classroom
  We all like to start our day on a good note. A cheery "good morning" goes a long way!

- Assist with daily attendance, homework, and dismissal routines, as well as next-day preparation such as posting a schedule
  Start to take initiative with these basic tasks. Your cooperating teacher will really appreciate the extra help.

- Become comfortable with the use of basic equipment and technology such as the copy machine, computer, book binder, overhead projector, interactive white boards, mobile devices, etc. (Technology will vary depending upon your placement so take advantage of all that is available.)
  With many basic tasks, the office staff will prove invaluable. The main office is the "heart" of the school. Befriending the office staff is a very smart move; you never know when you might be in a jam . . . a paper jam, that is!

- Help collect notices in the morning
  You will find that early in the morning can be quite hectic. It is helpful to have a "Morning Message" that gets the students working right away. Meanwhile, you can assist by collecting any permission slips, parent notes, or notices the students may bring in. Be sure to bring any important note to the teacher's attention right away.

- Monitor students in the hall

    You should help transition students to and from specialists, lunch, recess, assemblies, etc. by leading them quietly through the halls. Lead by example: stay to the right, keep quiet, etc.

- Jump into curriculum

    For example, start by assisting with spelling and/or grammar lessons; observe reading lessons/groups; formulate more questions about the curriculum – not just the what, but the how and why as well.

- KEEP BUSY!

    There will be times during the day when you will not be teaching, especially early on in your practicum. Your first goal should be to circulate and assist students as needed. Otherwise, make the most of these moments by asking your cooperating teacher, "How can I help you?" Here is a list of some helpful tasks.
    - Follow the teacher's model and an answer key to correct class/homework
    - Record grades
    - Accompany students on any errands or offer to run them yourself
    - Help organize classroom supplies
    - Offer to set up for the next lesson or clean up after a lesson
    - Distribute supplies, handouts, or books as needed
    - Make copies if needed
    - Wash overhead transparencies, whiteboards, etc.
    - Check the teacher's mailbox in the main office
    - Pass out any notices or offer to post online
    - Put up or take down bulletin board displays

TAKE NOTE!

    Now that you are more familiar with the routines of the classroom, begin to focus your attention more on the teaching practices such as timing and momentum.
    - Momentum/flow of lessons (directions, instruction, activity, closure)
    - Clarity and structure (clear goal, beginning, middle, end)
    - Timing
    - Flexibility (adaptation or revision of plans)
    - "Teachable moments"
    - Instructional practices (lecture, hands-on, group work, audiovisuals)
    - Technology
    - Teaching style
    - Inclusion of all learners
    - Formal or informal assessment

WEEKS 4-5: GETTING YOUR FEET EVEN WETTER

In addition to the above,

- Take over the daily routines

    Attendance, homework, dismissal, and basic next-day preparation should be automatic by this point. Routines are the small details that keep a classroom running smoothly.

- Take over spelling and/or grammar lessons

    Follow your cooperating teacher's modeling and the teacher's manuals to effectively teach these shorter lessons.

- Teach individual content area lessons (math, science, social studies, writing, whole-class reading)

    Review all lessons in advance and meet with your cooperating teacher to review the content as well as your plan for instruction. Be open to and even ask for feedback before, during, and after the actual lessons. Listening to advice early on will boost your confidence when you realize your own growth!

- Actively participate in small reading groups

    Small-group/guided reading instruction is a valuable tool in getting to know your students as readers. Pay close attention to how your cooperating teacher groups children, takes notes, asks questions, and varies instruction from group to group. ✦

- Maintain confidentiality and professionalism

    Remember that whenever you are observing and taking notes about a particular child or classroom experience, do not use real names. It is not professional to do so. In addition, you never know who may know the student(s) and what their relationship may be to students, teachers, or anyone in the school district in which you are working. It is always better to be safe than sorry.

TAKE NOTE!

    Look how far you've come already! By this point you probably know your class as a whole. How about as individuals with different learning styles and **special educational needs**?

- Choose a child in a Special Education Program to observe more closely
- Read his/her individualized education plan (IEP) noting the goals and objectives
- Get to know his/her learning style, strengths, and areas of need
- Note how the teacher(s) accommodate this special learner
- Attend consultation meetings with your cooperating teacher, the special education teacher, para-educator, and parent(s) when appropriate

WEEKS 6-7: HALF-TIME
In addition to the above,

- Teach sequential content area lessons

    It is important to experience the planning, execution, and follow-up of lessons not taught in "isolation." You will learn how to reflect and readjust the third and fourth lessons based on the first and second lessons. Flexibility is best learned with experience. What looks great on paper may look quite different in a real classroom. Be flexible!

- Collaborate with the teacher to plan small-group/guided reading

    Work with your cooperating practitioner to group children for small-group/guided reading. Find out the definite method to the "madness" of effectively matching students with the appropriate reading material. Also work together to plan, execute, and manage these flexible groupings. Note what the rest of the class is doing during this time.

- Become comfortable with the use of more advanced technology such as mobile devices, digital/video camera, projection machine (In-Focus), interactive whiteboard (SMART board, Mimeo), etc., but don't forget to familiarize yourself with the "good old-fashioned" TVs, DVDs, and even VCRs.

    Many times, the media or technology specialist can help you with this goal. If your education has exposed you to some of the newer technology, don't be afraid to teach the teacher!

- Expand your teaching/take-over time

    At this point, try taking over the teaching and classroom responsibilities for one full morning or afternoon each week. At first the students will look around for "the teacher." Remember, at these moments, YOU ARE THE TEACHER! Focus on your objectives. Students may ask you challenging or unexpected questions while your cooperating teacher is out of the room. Take deep breaths, and try not to get flustered. When appropriate, it's best to be honest and answer with those three magic words, "I'm not sure." Then just add on, "How can we find that out?"

- Step back and reflect

    As you approach the half-way mark, take the time to talk openly with your cooperating practitioner and your college supervisor about how things are going. Pat yourself on the back when it comes to things you have already learned and accomplished. Set new goals and ask for assistance with things upon which you'd still like to improve and/or areas in which you'd still like to grow.

<u>TAKE NOTE</u>!

By this point, you have had exposure to a variety of the <u>curriculum areas and</u> <u>assessment tools.</u>

CURRICULUM
- Take the time to research the Common Core and state standards (available online)
- Note the connections between content areas and language arts
- Pay attention to how the curriculum matches these guidelines
- Refer to and cite the state frameworks/standards when you plan your lessons

ASSESSMENT
- Observe and note effective informal and formal assessment for students' understanding of the material
- <u>Inquire about "high-stakes" testing in your state</u>
- <u>Seek out professionals such as the special education and reading teachers to</u> <u>ask more in-depth assessment questions</u>
- Take advantage of the professional resources around you
- Use all that you learn to improve upon your own teaching

WEEKS 8-10: MAKING YOUR MARK

In addition to the above,

- Focus on specific <u>management techniques</u> to maintain students' attention
  The focus is switching from how your cooperating practitioner teaches to how YOU teach. Keep in mind that how a classroom is managed determines how well students will learn. <u>Try out your own personal management style.</u>

- Plan and manage small-group/guided reading groups and activities
  When working with small groups, don't forget <u>"the rest of the class."</u> All students should be engaged in meaningful activities that they can complete independently.
  Devise a <u>question-answering strategy for those students who may need help while</u> <u>you're occupied with a small group.</u> For example, try the <u>"ask three before me"</u> method where students can ask up to three classmates any question they may have. Usually the very first student can clear up any confusion!

- Expand your teaching/take-over time

    Take over the classroom for at least one full day per week. Learn how to smoothly transition from one subject to the next. This includes set-up and clean-up of any materials you may need. This also includes transitioning the students to any specialists and managing your planning time while they are out of the room.

- Create informal and formal assessment for students' understanding

    Use that textbook knowledge! Remember learning in classes about anecdotal records, "dip sticking," objective vs. subjective assessment, and even pre-testing? Try them out now! Create and vary assessment for all content areas. Discuss your ideas with your cooperating practitioner both in advance and post-grading. Then assess yourself: Did you get the results you expected? Do you need to re-teach or revisit any material? Was your assessment too basic or too challenging? How clear were your directions?

- Begin preparing for your take-over period

    Following your college and/or state requirements, outline your objectives and begin planning and preparing for your take-over period. It will be here before you know it! Keep in mind that you will be taking over FULL RESPONSIBILITIES in the classroom during your take-over period. Start planning early and you'll cover all your bases!

TAKE NOTE!

Have you noticed the various forms of communication teachers utilize each and every day? How does your cooperating teacher formally and informally communicate with parents, students, colleagues, and even you? Take the time to think positively as you send your own communication out. (Again, don't forget to have someone proofread your work – it is a reflection of you both personally and professionally!)

- Generate positive rewards, comments, notes, and feedback to students and/or parents
- Communicate with parents through your own contribution to a "weekly update" of classroom happenings
- Participate in or observe report card conferences if possible
- Invite parents into the classroom for a special event you are planning
- Send notes to teachers in the school requesting observation time in their classrooms
- Schedule as many different classroom visits as you can, carefully selecting the most meaningful observation times (post-take-over period is best)

WEEKS 11-12: THE HOME STRETCH
In addition to the above,

- Expand your teaching/take-over time

    Try taking over the classroom for two or more consecutive days. This will help prepare you (and your students) for a week or more of full responsibilities. You will be amazed that the students no longer look for "the teacher" during these times. YOU ARE THE TEACHER!

- Invite observers and feedback

    In addition to your college supervisor, you may want to invite the principal or assistant principal to observe you teaching during your take-over week. Write a friendly note with suggested times, but remain flexible. Ask respectfully for a few minutes of follow-up afterward. Not only can you get great feedback, but there's a chance you'll be making an impression on a future employer!

TAKE NOTE!

Focus on **preparation and collaboration** as take-over week rapidly approaches!
- Collaborate with your cooperating practitioner, the reading specialist, and special education teacher as needed to complete all planning and preparation, including modification for any special needs and all assessment.
- Spare no detail during preparation: make all necessary copies, label everything, reserve necessary technology, arrange seating, etc.
- Be extra-thorough if you've decided to invite parents into the classroom

WEEK 13: THE GRAND FINALE

- Complete your take-over period

    During this period you will assume the full responsibilities of the classroom. Incorporate the instructional strategies and management techniques you have acquired during student teaching. (Although you are "in charge," do not hesitate to ask for any assistance as needed and to stay in close communication with your cooperating practitioner.)

- Be confident and flexible . . . and HAVE FUN!

TAKE NOTE!

The most successful educators have earned that title by being **reflective**. They not only celebrate what goes well, but constantly consider how they can better their instruction to improve their students' learning.
- Reflect upon and note how your take-over period is going each day
- Make any changes necessary to improve the students' learning

WEEK 14: THE LAST HURRAH!

The final week is bittersweet. You may be surprised at how attached you've become to the students. Be proud of your accomplishments and realize not only how much you have taught them, but how much they have taught you!

- Come full circle on any teaching
  Although take-over period is technically over, fulfill any teaching obligations. Perhaps there was a school cancellation, fire drill, or other interruption. Or maybe you just needed to adjust your lessons to better fit the students' learning. No matter the circumstance, follow through with your professional teaching responsibilities. Believe it or not, you are making an impression until the day you are done – and beyond!

- Keep any appointments you have made
  Observe other grade-level classrooms or meet with any specialists with whom you have set appointments.

TAKE NOTE!

In these final days, spend your time professionally putting the finishing touches on everything as **closure**.

- Complete your professional portfolio
- Review and finalize state and college requirements
- Give your cooperating practitioner copies of lessons, etc. if you haven't done so already
- Compose a heartfelt thank-you/good-bye letter addressed to parents and students
- Plan a final activity with the students
- Circulate to properly and genuinely thank those who made the school a warm and welcoming place for you
- Write personal notes to those who directly contributed to a successful once-in-a-lifetime student teaching experience
- End your experience the way it began . . . on a positive and professional note

CONGRATULATIONS!!!

LEARN YOUR LESSON:
QUALITY LESSON PLANNING

The ultimate goal of planning a quality lesson is that it will result in quality learning. Although the actual learning is of utmost importance, it is also important be able to compose a formal lesson plan in order to professionally communicate your goals. Whether you are planning an original lesson or one from set curriculum, you will need to consider many things as you plan: the specific curriculum content, clear student objectives, effective and varied instructional strategies, appropriate forms of assessment, and use of available technology. Let's take a closer look at the basics of each of these categories.

KNOW YOUR STUFF
Familiarizing yourself with state standards, curriculum content, and student objectives

So you have to teach a lesson, where should you begin? Rule #1 in lesson planning is to begin with the END in mind! What does this mean? The "end" is the ultimate content learning goal you have for your students. Districts (and teachers) use documents such as state standards (or frameworks) to help select grade-level curriculum and to guide teachers in planning effective lessons. Today, all content that is taught should be directly related to such standards. So, when you're planning a lesson consider: How is what I am planning to teach related to the state standards and frameworks?

Familiarizing yourself with state standards will give you a better understanding of the grade-level content expected to be taught. Remember, you're not expected to be an expert in all curriculum areas. There are many ways to brush up on the content you're expected to teach. Use your resources. Ask your cooperating practitioner for advice and for materials. He/she will be able to provide you with his/her personal experience and expertise as well as any related teacher manuals, textbooks, trade books, and technology that supplement the curriculum. The media specialist can also help you find background information and potential teaching tools.

TECHNOLOGY TIPS:
Since technology in the 21st century is continuously evolving, the best tip is to take advantage of whatever technology is currently available to you. When used selectively, reliable, research-based Internet resources are an endless source of information.

With an understanding of the general grade-level content under your belt, you need to identify specifically what you want your students to learn and/or be able to do by the end of the lesson.

ACTION!
Using <u>vivid verbs</u> in your student objectives

Objectives are what you want your students to know and/or be able to do by the end of the lesson. Student objectives may focus on knowledge (specific curriculum content), skills (such as cutting or highlighting), or attitudes (values). It is best to write these objectives in clear and complete sentences. Use strong action verbs to help you state your expectations, and consider varying your levels of thinking from basic (define, list, match) to complex (compare, contrast, justify).

<u>KNOWLEDGE EXAMPLES:</u>
Students will be able to . . .
- *categorize* materials as solids, liquids or gases.
- *label* a map of the original 13 colonies.
- *sequence* the planets in their order from the sun.

<u>SKILL EXAMPLES:</u>
Students will be able to . . .
- *draw* an acute angle.
- *write* a science lab report.
- *create* an electric circuit using a battery and wire.

<u>ATTITUDE EXAMPLES:</u>
Students will be able to . . .
- *defend* Columbus's title as "Discoverer of America."
- *conserve* energy in their own homes.
- *express* their personal opinions about presidential candidates.

After you have determined your student objectives, the next step is to decide how you will design your lesson in order for the students to meet these goals.

MIX IT UP
Incorporating various instructional strategies to meet the needs of diverse learners

There are many different ways to teach children the content. At this point in your lesson planning, you need to think about how to best match your instructional practices to your objectives and to the diverse learning styles of your students. You also need to prepare appropriate materials and consider the learning environment that will best support the activities you choose. Although it may seem overwhelming at first, this is the exciting part of the lesson, where your creativity can truly shine!

YOUR OVERALL APPROACH TO INSTRUCTIONAL PRACTICES

When choosing an instructional approach for a specific lesson, you will need to take many factors into account. First, consider the content you are teaching and the role both you and the students will be taking. Will you be teaching a hands-on science lesson during which the students will be experimenting with materials, or leading a grammar lesson during which the students will be reading a selection looking for various types of punctuation? Will the students be working in groups, independently, or with partners? Will your students be paired randomly or cooperatively? Next, you need to consider the different learning styles of your students. Will your students be best engaged when the information is presented to them visually or verbally? Will you enhance your lesson by using technology? Will your students be more attentive seated at their desks or seated in a common meeting area?

To acquire a variety of instructional strategies and learn when to use them, you should first become familiar with those that your cooperating teacher uses. Carefully observe your cooperating teacher in action as he/she teaches lessons in the different content areas throughout the day. After a specific lesson, ask him/her to share with you why he/she decided to use a specific approach with the students. Take notes and reflect upon what you see so that you are more comfortable with the strategies as you begin taking on more of the teaching responsibilities.

What's that, you want to try new instructional strategies with your students? Student teaching is a great time to try some innovative techniques. After all, your student teaching practicum is a safe place to "get your feet wet." However, before you begin experimenting with new instructional strategies, it's a good idea to start with strategies with which your students are already familiar, then slowly integrate your own personal teaching techniques.

After considering the overall instructional approach you will take, you are ready to complete planning a lesson with three clear key components (an opening, a body, and a closing) that will have the students learning – hook, line, and sinker!

HOOK: STARTING A LESSON

How you introduce the lesson is a very important first step as it is the way to "hook" your students. The introduction to your lesson should not only grab your students' attention, but should also activate their prior knowledge about the topic, surface any misconceptions they may have, and clearly state the lesson objectives.

To accomplish these goals, your opener might include brainstorming of prior knowledge by having the students write a brief response to a sentence starter. By doing so, each student will have the opportunity to think about the topic, including what he/she may already know as well as what he/she would like to know. Taking a few minutes to think about the topic in advance gives all students an equal chance to share their responses and participate in a meaningful class discussion. You will learn what your students may already know and/or what misconceptions they may have during this whole-group discussion or even by circulating to review individual student responses. This information is very valuable as it should guide the direction of your lesson.

Another important part of your opener is to state your lesson objectives. As mentioned previously, if everyone is clear on the learning outcomes and the plan of action, greater learning can and will take place.

The following is an example of one way to end the introductory portion of the lesson:
So far we have brainstormed a list of ideas we think we know about _____.
The reason we did this is because today we are going to be learning _____ and _____. We are going to do this by _____and _____. At the end of lesson, I will be checking to see if we learned the new information by having you _____.

LINE: TEACHING A LESSON
After "hooking" your students into the lesson, it is time to reel them in by getting them actively engaged in their learning. Once again, the strategies you use are dependent on the subject area that you are teaching and the specific objectives for the lesson. Research shows that children learn best by doing, so what is most important here is that you get your students directly involved in the lesson by providing them with hands-on activities that allow them to explore, discover, experiment, and create. (This is what is referred to as a constructivist approach to learning.)

Keep your students' learning styles in mind while planning this portion of your lesson. Using graphic organizers as you teach is a great way to involve students who learn best through visual modes. Having students take notes using a graphic organizer as you present important information is one way to keep your students actively engaged. In addition, you may want to differentiate the activity so that students can build their knowledge and skills at their own pace. For example, some learners may use a word bank to complete a diagram of a pond snail's habitat, while others may follow step-by-step guidelines for recording their own observations about pond snails in their natural habitat, and still others may do online database research to write a detailed report comparing and contrasting the habitats of pond snails and land snails. This is also the time to incorporate any modifications and/or accommodations for any students with special needs, so be sure to consult with any special education teachers and/or para-educators who may be working with students in your classroom.

The multiple intelligences can also be incorporated effectively into engaging and worthwhile learning activities. Try integrating art, music, or physical activity into your lesson. For example, try some exercises to pep up your students' learning, like having them march out their math facts or do jumping jacks to the states and capitals. Your kinesthetic students will surely get a "kick" out of this!

As you plan, don't forget the instructional details of your lesson. Consider the speaking tone and pace you will use, the clarity of your directions, your movement and circulation around the room, the timing and momentum of the lesson, and the physical arrangement of the classroom. In addition, don't overlook another very important aspect of lesson planning – overplanning. You should always have something worthwhile for students to do if they finish the main activity early, so plan ahead. Yet while it may be much better to have too much planned than not enough, another good tip is to chunk your lesson into smaller sections so that if you run out of time (or there's a fire drill during the lesson!), you can stop at an appropriate point and successfully continue the lesson at a later time. Always think ahead!

SINKER: CLOSING A LESSON

So, you taught all that you'd planned to teach and the activity is complete. The lesson is over, right? NO WAY! The closing part of your lesson is a critical time for your students to make some of the most meaningful learning connections.

At this time you should ask your students some thought-provoking questions like:
- Why is it important to learn about _____?
- How is what we learned today used in the world?
- What type of careers might require this type of knowledge?
- What is the most important thing you learned today? Why?
- What is one question you still have about _____ ?
- How is _____ like _____ ? How are they different?
- How would you summarize today's lesson in three words? Two? One?
- How would you explain today's lesson to a student who was absent? To a younger sibling?
- Based on today's lesson, what predictions do you have about the next lesson? Why?

The closing is also the time to have your students share and summarize some of the most important concepts they have learned. An effective strategy to use at the end of a lesson is to have students utilize graphic organizers or keep notebooks in which they reflect upon their learning by making real-world connections and explaining what they just learned in their own words. This is a great time to integrate additional interactive technology to further enhance powerful teaching and learning.

P.S. GET YOUR STUFF TOGETHER: ORGANIZING APPROPRIATE MATERIALS
There is nothing worse than a lesson's momentum being put on hold because a teacher needs to stop and prepare materials! Preparation and organization of materials should all be done well in advance. As you are writing your lesson plan, be sure to consider and list all of the supplies you will need in order for the students to complete the learning activities and assignments. Organize the materials so that they are easily accessible

when you need them. Have extras on hand for those "just in case" incidents: extra pencils, extra handouts, etc. Also be sure to gather in advance the appropriate teaching materials you need including any technology and/or other audiovisual aids. You can never be too prepared!

TESTING 1, 2, 3
Including appropriate assessment

Another important piece of planning your lesson is the assessment you choose. Assessment is a way of collecting data about student progress, and there are many ways to do so. Review the following assessment subtopics before choosing the appropriate method(s). Remember that the big question to ask is, "How will I know that my students have met my learning objectives?" ALWAYS refer back to the student objectives when designing or choosing assessment, and ALWAYS use the assessment data you collect to drive your future instruction.

INFORMAL VERSUS FORMAL ASSESSMENT
- Formal assessment provides teachers with a systematic way to measure student progress and usually has specific expectations. Many times, formal assessment takes the form of paper-and-pencil assignments such as teacher- or company-created tests, quizzes, reports, or projects.
- Informal assessment tools may not have specific guidelines. Anecdotal records, observations, group discussions, reading logs, student-teacher conferences, oral responses, and class participation are forms of informal assessment.

For example, if your objective is that students will be able to recall 20 basic addition facts in one minute, your formal assessment may be a timed fact test. An informal assessment for the same objective may be a whole-class fast-paced slate assessment of addition facts.

OBJECTIVE VERSUS SUBJECTIVE ASSESSMENT
- When looking for concrete answers, think about including objective questions in the form of true/false, multiple choice, fill-in-the-blank, and/or matching as well as short answer and/or essay. For example, if your objective is that students will be able to identify the setting of a story, an objective assessment question may be: The novel *My Brother Sam is Dead* is set in the town of _____ in the colony of _____.
- For subjective assessment, opinions and application of ideas and concepts are usually abstract as opposed to concrete answers. For subjective assessment, consider inferential short answer and/or essay questions. For example, if your objective is that students will be able to evaluate a character's decision or action, a subjective assessment question may be: In *My Brother Sam is Dead*, evaluate Tim's plan to outsmart the cowboys.

When choosing or creating formal assessment, consider varying the types and levels of questions asked. Also decide if your assessment will be a shorter quiz or a longer test.

PROCESS VERSUS PRODUCT ASSESSMENT

- Sometimes you will need to assess a process. This may take the form of a pre-writing graphic organizer or a checklist of science experiment procedures. For example, if your objective is that students will be able to cooperate with science partners, your assessment may be informal observation of group work or a partnership's self-assessment checklist.

- Other times it is an end product that is being evaluated. This may be a traditionally graded end-of-chapter test or a book project scored using a rubric. For example, if your objective is that students will be able to sequence the planets in their order from the sun, your assessment may take the form of a blank map of our solar system or manipulate a model of our solar system. As you gain more experience assigning and grading end products like projects, consider offering the students choices. For example, let them creatively express their learning by producing a music video, Power Point, puppet show, movie, or game board instead of having everyone writing a standard book report.

ASSESSMENT BEYOND A SINGLE LESSON

Although you are matching your assessment to the objectives of a single lesson, remember that student assessment may be cumulative and should fit into the "bigger picture." Inquire in advance about how your lesson fits into a theme, chapter, or unit. Also ask your cooperating teacher about his/her assessment procedures beyond a single lesson such as:

- Varying assessment tools to create a balanced approach to assessment
- Grading assessment and recording results
- Providing students with written and/or verbal feedback on assessment
- Communicating with parents about assessment as needed: phone, note, conference, email
- Translating assessment into report card grades or measuring progress toward meeting the grade-level standards
- Using ongoing or alternative assessment such as portfolios
- Considering the role of "high-stakes" assessment or state-mandated testing

Although assessment is presented here as a tool to measure student progress, remember that assessment should also drive future instruction. If you notice that students did not do well on an assessment, reevaluate the situation. Is it time to review the key concepts for further understanding, or should you move on to the next lesson knowing that the key concepts will resurface in a spiral effect?

A FINAL NOTE ON LESSON PLANS

You do not need to write a formal lesson plan for every lesson you teach. However, you should always type a complete lesson plan whenever you will be formally observed. These professional documents serve as pre- and post-conference guides and will become an essential part of your professional portfolio. In addition, lesson plans are the best form of preparation and reflection for you as an educator.

While it may seem obvious that the formal plan of action helps you prepare for the lesson, it is always a good idea to stop and reflect after implementing a lesson as well. Make notes and/or changes to your lesson plan after you've evaluated the effectiveness of the lesson yourself, gotten feedback from someone who observed the lesson (cooperating practitioner, college supervisor, etc.), or even asked the students. Since they experienced the lesson from a different perspective, the students often give the most thoughtful comments and suggestions!

You should always follow the lesson plan format set by your college. However, with any formal lesson plan to be shared with others, you will probably need to include the following essential parts in your written document to prove you have "learned your lesson"!

PARTS OF A LESSON PLAN
- Title
- Subject/Content Area
- Level
- Time Frame
- Objectives
- Common Core/State Standard Connections
- Materials
- Procedures
- Modifications/Accommodations
- Assessment

SAMPLE FORMAL LESSON PLAN

TITLE: Liquid Drop Races
SUBJECT: Science
LEVEL: Grade 1
TIME FRAME: 30 minutes

OBJECTIVES:
- Students will be able to predict which of two liquids will travel down the slick surface faster.
- Students will be able to test their predictions by conducting a drop race test.
- Students will be able to record, discuss, and compare their results.
- Students will be able to cooperate with their science partners.

COMMON CORE/MASSACHUSETTS STANDARDS CONNECTIONS
Physical Science Grades preK-2
- Sort objects by observable properties such as size, shape, color, weight, and texture.
- Identify objects and materials as solid, liquid, or gas.
- Recognize that liquids take the shape of their container.

Connections to First Grade Curriculum:
This science lesson is adapted from the Science and Technology for Children (STC) Solids and Liquids Unit adopted by the Spring Valley Public School District.

MATERIALS:
For each student:
- Science journal - Racing Drops Record Sheet
- Pencil

For science partners:
- 2 white plastic taster spoons
- 1 plastic tray
- 2 cups of different liquids (shampoo, oil, water, glue)

PROCEDURES:
1.   To activate prior knowledge, the teacher will begin by asking the children to think about a rainy day and asking the following questions:
    - Do you ever watch rain fall on a window?
    - If so, what does the rain look like as it hits the window?
    - Describe what the rain does after hitting the window.

23

2. At this time, the teacher will "hook" the children by telling them that today's science lesson is like watching rain on a window, except that they will be using at least two of the four liquids (water, oil, shampoo, glue) instead of rainwater.

3. To begin, the teacher will review some of the results of previous tests conducted with the liquids. More specifically, the teacher will pose the questions:
   - Which liquid moved fastest on the waxed paper?
   - Which liquid flowed slowest in the bag?

4. Next, the teacher will inform the students that they will be conducting drop race tests with the liquids. Their experiment will be to find out which liquid travels down a slick surface faster.

5. Then the students will be dismissed to their pre-assigned partners/work groups and asked to make predictions about the two liquids that they will be testing. (The liquids will be at their stations.) The children will need to write the names of the two liquids at the top of their record sheet prior to conducting the test.

6. The students will then place a spoonful of each liquid on the flat surface close to one end of the tray. The teacher will model and inform the students that each liquid drop should be about the size of a nickel.

7. Before the races begin, the teacher will alert the students that some of the races will go very quickly so they need to be sure to carefully observe what is happening. On command, students will tilt their trays to a complete vertical position, with the drops at the top.

8. As soon as the race ends the students will be directed to circle the name of the liquid that won the race.

9. If time allows, the students may conduct another race to retest their findings or to test the additional two liquids. They may use the backside of the tray.

10. After partners complete the tests, they will clean their work areas. Then the teacher will invite students to the rug area to record the findings on a central drop race chart.

11. The teacher will facilitate an inquiry discussion by posing several questions to the students:
    - Were you surprised by any of the results? If so, which ones?
    - Were your results the same as your predictions? If not, then what changed? Why?

MODIFICATIONS/ACCOMODATIONS:
Two students will have the support of special education assistants. Modifications will be made based on their IEP goals.

ASSESSMENT:
Informal Assessment:
The teacher will observe the students as they are conducting the test and discussing the results of the test.

Formal Assessment:
The record keeping/data collection of the individual record sheet, Drop Races, will serve as a formal assessment.

The children will be assessed on the following criteria:
- A prediction is recorded prior to conducting the actual test
- The actual results of the test are drawn on the record sheet
- The liquids are properly labeled
- The name of the liquid that won the drop race is circled
- The written information is neat and organized

S.O.S.: WHO'S IN CONTROL ANYWAY?
EFFECTIVE CLASSROOM MANAGEMENT

One of the greatest teaching challenges is developing an effective classroom management system. Teacher preparation courses teach us the theories behind learning and the content which we will be teaching; however, as equally important as it is, a course on how to MANAGE a classroom is usually not offered.

Classroom management refers to all of the organizational tasks and planning a teacher does in order to prepare a student-centered learning environment as well as the management of keeping students on task. An effective classroom management system often takes years of development, but your student teaching practicum is the best place to start. With this in mind, be sure to observe, learn, and use from your cooperating practitioner as many classroom management strategies as you can. What you will begin to see is that some techniques are subtle, that is, they are implemented "behind the scenes" often without the students even knowing (desk arrangement, placement of students, organization of materials), while other strategies are very obvious, such as a posted schedule, class expectations, daily procedures, and a positive incentive program.

CLASSROOM MANAGEMENT DETERMINES HOW WELL STUDENTS WILL LEARN
Learning how to manage a room full of students takes a positive attitude and lots of effort. With effective classroom management, the actual teaching becomes easier! A simple rule of thumb is to reinforce students' positive behaviors in order to help diminish the negative ones. Remember, there is good in every child!

FINDING THE GOOD IN EVERY CHILD
The ultimate goal is for all students to be intrinsically motivated to learn and follow classroom and school expectations. Sometimes an incentive program can complement the caring classroom community. During your take-over period, you may try to establish such a classroom incentive program. (Be sure to get approval from your cooperating teacher beforehand.) For example, explain to your students that for every positive behavior you "catch" them demonstrating, they will be able to put a marble (jellybean, scoop of popcorn kernels, etc.) into a jar. If the jar fills before take-over period is complete, you and your students can celebrate in a special way.

Another motivational idea is to create a raffle jar. When someone is "caught" doing a positive behavior, have the student write his/her name on a slip of paper and put it in the jar. At the end of the week, you can draw a name (or names) from the "positive people jar," and that child is rewarded in a special way. These rewards can include a certificate, pencil, sticker, other small token, or simply a congratulatory handshake or round of applause.

IS ANYONE LISTENING TO ME?

You may lose the attention of your students at any point during your teaching. Don't worry, it happens to the best of us! What should you do? Many student teachers, and even some experienced teachers, continue to teach, hoping that they can recapture the attention of their students. However, trying to teach over the chattering is not effective. By doing so, it sends the message that it is acceptable to talk when another person is speaking.

If you are trying to regain the attention of your students during a lesson, some effective strategies to try are to make a patterned hand clap and have students echo it, shut off the lights, ring a set of wind chimes, use a tuning wand, or signal your students by using a certain gesture.

BAG OF TRICKS

Think of an effective classroom management system as your "bag of tricks." You need to have lots and lots of strategies in your bag as there is not just ONE management strategy that works for every student and/or behavior! Your student teaching practicum allows you the opportunity to learn and observe a variety of effective strategies with which to start your own bag.

Here are some other classroom management suggestions to help keep your students focused and your student-teaching experience a positive one.

TOP TEN TIPS FOR EFFECTIVE CLASSROOM MANAGEMENT

1. Arrange the classroom to maximize student learning for the lesson you are about to teach. Should the desks face forward, be in rows or groups, etc.?

2. Have all of your materials ready (including extras just in case).

3. Get all of your students' attention BEFORE you begin a lesson.

    NOTE: If something happens in the classroom or out in the schoolyard that may need to be addressed with the students, don't wait to address it. It is best to stop your teaching, take a few minutes to discuss the situation and help the students problem-solve other ways the situation could have been handled. Taking a few minutes to do this prior to beginning a lesson will save you lots of time trying to refocus the students all through your lesson!

4.   Be clear; let your students know what they will be doing, what the expectations are, and what the final product should look like.

5.   Don't talk too much! Use no more than 10-15 minutes of class to introduce the activity, then get your students working.

6.   Continue to move around the classroom to make connections with your students; give a gentle shoulder tap or other signal to any students that may need redirecting.

7.   Catch your students being "good" and doing what they should be doing; be sure to recognize, reinforce, and reward these positive behaviors.

8.   Keep ALL students actively involved. For example, while one student is reading aloud or presenting, have the other students take notes on important facts they hear. Also, technology can be a super motivator. Try inviting students up to the interactive white board.

9.   Take advantage of those "teachable moments" that occur throughout the day. Many times the best learning is unplanned!

10.   And remember . . . ALWAYS keep your sense of humor!

ALL EYES ON YOU:
CONFERENCING AND BEING OBSERVED

Remember how difficult it was during the early days of your practicum when you stood in front and taught a class with 20 pairs of eyes on you, not to mention the eyes of your cooperating teacher! With that under your belt, the real pressure is on. It is time for your supervisor to visit and to formally observe you teach a lesson . . . how nerve-wracking!

Take a deep breath. Chances are your supervisor was in fact once a teacher, and had to go through the same process as you are going through now. The sooner you get comfortable being observed, the easier it will be and the more you will learn about yourself as a teacher.

INITIAL CONFERENCE
Before your first official observation by your supervisor, you will need to arrange for an initial conference with both your cooperating teacher and your supervisor. This three-way meeting should be held within the first two weeks of school. Ask both your cooperating teacher and college supervisor for convenient meeting dates and times. Be flexible and accommodate their schedules as best as possible. This first meeting is a great time to show them your professionalism by making the initial introductions and being well-prepared.

Your college will provide you with the practicum requirements and necessary paperwork to be completed and submitted to the state for your initial licensure. Have this paperwork on hand at your initial three-way conference, and mark off all of the locations that require a college supervisor and/or cooperating practitioner signature. Also, record in advance any questions that you may have and ask them at this meeting so that everyone is on the same page.

This initial meeting is only the first of many. Your supervisor will need to observe you for a minimum of 3 times during the semester, so while you are all sitting together, try to decide upon all of your meeting dates. Although it may seem too early to do so, their schedules (and yours) will fill up quickly. Having these dates arranged in advance will help you to best prepare and map out the upcoming semester. Keep in mind that the cooperating teacher should be present at post-observation conferences, so suggest scheduling observation lessons right before a preparatory period or lunch break so your teacher can join.

Every college/cooperating teacher may approach the practicum requirement of a take-over week(s) differently. Therefore, this first meeting is also a time to start discussing and scheduling your take-over time. Ask early about your cooperating teacher's expectations for you during that week. By midway through your practicum, confirm what curriculum you'll be teaching during that week and if there are any special events for which you'll need to plan (field trips, holidays, assemblies, etc.) Early and open communication during your initial conference helps to make for a smooth semester.

PRE-OBSERVATION CONFERENCE
To prepare for your very first observation, review your lesson plan with your cooperating teacher well in advance of the actual lesson. Listen openly to any suggestions that he/she may have to offer and make adjustments accordingly. Then have a copy of your formal lesson plan ready for your college supervisor.

Some colleges require you to have a pre-observation conference with your supervisor to discuss your lesson plan prior to teaching it. This is a great practice to get into, so if it is not a requirement yet your supervisor is willing to meet, go for it! The more times you go over your lesson plan, especially with others, the clearer it will be in your mind and the more relaxed you will be while you are teaching it. Who knows, you may even ENJOY teaching it!

Whether you are meeting for the pre-observation conference or for the observation itself, it is respectful to meet your supervisor at the main office and escort him/her to your classroom whenever possible. Look her/him in the eye and offer a firm handshake. As you enter the classroom, reintroduce your supervisor to your cooperating teacher, and if it is appropriate, to your students as well.

OBSERVATION ROUND ONE
You're ready to teach! Go about this formal observation as you would any other day of teaching: your first priority is to focus on the students. If you are well-prepared and rehearsed, the lesson is sure to go smoothly (easier said than done, right?). Be clear with your objectives and procedures, and just do your best. To help you stay focused, have a copy of your lesson plan nearby and refer to it periodically. Some student teachers have even made themselves notes on index cards to help keep them on track. Although it may seem like an eternity, the time will actually fly by! So watch the clock to be time-efficient.

So it wasn't perfect? Mistakes happen! If you do happen to make a minor mistake during your lesson, just keep on teaching and try not to think about it. Chances are, no one will notice. On the other hand, if you make an error that needs to be addressed (such as saying there are 40 United States instead of 50), recognize that you made a mistake and either correct it yourself or ask your students for the correct response. By being proactive like this, you are modeling very important life skills for your students: nobody is perfect, and everyone makes mistakes!

After the lesson is finished, take another deep breath and relax. You did it! Now it's time to reflect and to hear feedback on your lesson from your college supervisor and/or cooperating teacher.

POST-OBSERVATION CONFERENCE

Your conference time with your supervisor is very important. Your supervisor will help you to reflect upon your lesson and your teaching practices. Remember that it is part of his/her position to assist you as you become a teacher. He/she will give you some positive feedback as well as advice and suggestions, so be prepared. Share the best part(s) of the lesson and celebrate this success. Ask for his/her thoughts on parts of the lesson that didn't go so well. To help assess the lesson, look at student output together. Then don't forget to take a sample ☆ of a student's work to display in your portfolio.

Your supervisor may take notes and/or fill out a rubric as you teach and as you conference depending on your college/state requirements. Your cooperating teacher should be included in this conference to some degree. Together, the three of you can discuss the things that went well during the lesson (strengths) in addition to the things that didn't go so well (areas that need improvement). During the conference, ask for advice on how you can further develop in those areas before your next lesson observation. At the conclusion of the meeting, thank the two of them for their support and time and confirm with them the date and time of your next formal observation.

OBSERVATION ROUND TWO

Teaching during your second observation will feel much more natural than during your first one since you have much more teaching experience now. Nevertheless, you still need to be well-prepared and professional. Be proud of the praise about your progress thus far, yet still listen openly and take advantage of any advice and suggestions being offered.

By the second (or midway) lesson observation, you should have a collection of student work for use in your portfolio. As you conference with your supervisor, share these samples and discuss why you chose them to represent important aspects of your student teaching. Go over any practicum-related assignments that may still be unclear. Be sure that you are up-to-date on all of your practicum paperwork and confirm your next and/or final lesson observation with your cooperating teacher and supervisor.

OBSERVATION ROUND THREE

This observation can be a bittersweet one for student teachers because it represents the end of the practicum. By this point, you should be teaching for the majority of the school day and the students should feel like your own. Typically this observation is scheduled during your take-over week so that your supervisor has the opportunity to see how you handle complete classroom responsibility. Allow for some time either before or after your lesson to review all of the necessary final paperwork and to showcase some of the highlights of your take-over week.

This is a time for you to shine: demonstrate how you have grown into an effective classroom teacher!

FINAL OBSERVATION TIP If you tend to get nervous about being observed, inviting lots of people in to watch you teach is great experience.   If your cooperating teacher approves, invite other student teachers, other teachers, and/or the building principal to observe you at different points throughout your practicum. It's a great way to learn and grow. Plus you never know, someday you may be asking them to write you letters of recommendation.

MIRROR, MIRROR:
THOUGHTFULLY REFLECTING UPON YOUR TEACHING

When you look in a mirror you probably subconsciously think about different ways to improve your physical being. If reflection can lead to an improvement in appearance, just imagine what it can lead to with regards to improving daily teaching practices. Reflective thinking has the power to change an average lesson into an exemplary one and transform a good teacher into an excellent one.

A PLACE TO START: REFLECTING WITH YOUR COOPERATING TEACHER

It can be overwhelming trying to reflect upon every aspect of your teaching at once. (However, by continuously employing good reflective practices, it will eventually come naturally.) To keep it manageable during your practicum, start by focusing on just ONE aspect of teaching at a time. Suggested topics include, but are not limited to: classroom management, timing and momentum, special education, curriculum and assessment, use of available technology, communication, and preparation and collaboration. Spend time observing the students and your cooperating practitioner with these topics in mind. Jot any related notes and/or questions in a journal, then discuss them with the teacher to get a feel for how reflective thinking truly can improve instruction.

For example,

- Why did you rearrange the desks for this science activity? Were the students placed randomly or was it pre-planned? How did you decide?
- What do you do when you haven't finished the lesson, yet it is time for lunch?
- I noticed from the students' math quizzes that many of them didn't understand the concept of area. How do you know when to stop to further review a concept or to move on to the next topic?
- Why do a few of the students have different materials for tomorrow's social studies note-taking lesson? How did you learn to modify the curriculum or to make accommodations for a student's special needs?
- Have you ever taught lessons that didn't go as well as you had planned? What did you do to improve them for the next time?

You will find that teachers DO have reasons for the decisions they make, but most teachers do not usually verbalize WHY they do certain things or react in certain ways. By asking thoughtful questions and collaborating with your cooperating teacher, you will discover and observe firsthand the power of reflective thinking.

YOUR TURN: A SIMPLE EXERCISE

How do you begin to reflect upon yourself as a teacher? Start simple. Each week of your student teaching, complete the following sentences in a reflection journal:

- Three things I am most proud of . . .
- Three things I still need to work on . . .

These simple sentence starters will get you reflecting upon, and therefore improving, your instruction . . . just like with the mirror! Then take the time to discuss your ideas with your cooperating practitioner and even with other student teachers. Keep these notes and refer back to them each week as your practicum progresses. You will be amazed by how much you learn and grow through such a seemingly simple reflective exercise.

THE BIGGER PICTURE: IMPROVING YOURSELF IN MULTIPLE ASPECTS OF INSTRUCTION

During your practicum (and even into your first years as a teacher), with so much to learn and do, you often move from one lesson to the next, without giving too much thought to its outcome. You tend to be just relieved and grateful that it is finished, moving on to the next thing without a second thought. That is until you discover the power of reflective thinking.

Without reflective thinking from the start, it may be years into your teaching before you find yourself making "notes to self" on the sides of your plan book or posting sticky notes inside your manuals to remind you of things you want to change about the lesson the next time you teach it. Until you begin to listen to yourself and react to self-thoughts about your teaching practices and lessons, nothing will change. Each time you do the lesson, you'll keep doing it the same way and say, "Well, it's just the way I've always done it." However, if you become reflective in your teaching practices as soon as you begin, you will be at an incredible advantage, and more importantly, so will your students!

You cannot be expected to reflect upon every aspect of every lesson every day. You would spend all of your time reflecting and not teaching! Do your best to select different curriculum areas, parts of the day, and/or instructional strategies upon which to reflect. As this becomes a more natural process, you will learn and grow as a teacher.

QUESTION YOURSELF

At the end of a lesson, spend a minute or two to think about what just occurred. Ask yourself a FEW of the following questions. Then make clear notes in your plan book or teacher's manual for the next time. (In theory, mental notes are great, too, but with so much going on, rarely can a teacher sustain mental notes! And remember that "next time" is usually a whole year away!)

- How did the lesson go overall?
- How did the implementation of the lesson compare to my expectations?
- What part of the lesson makes me most proud?
- Which part was most effective? Why?

- What part of the lesson was least effective? Why?
- What went particularly well? (There's always something!)
- What part didn't go as well as planned? (There's always something!)
- What aspect(s) of the lesson will I definitely keep the same next time? Why?
- What aspect(s) of the lesson will I definitely change the next time? Why?
- What can I do to improve this lesson in the future?
- How did I feel about my choice of: teaching strategies, sequencing, timing, momentum, modifications/accommodations, management, technology integration, materials, visual aids, organization, etc.?

Interestingly enough, two very popular interview questions are:
- Tell us about a lesson that you feel went well. How do you know that it went well, and why do you think that it went so well?
- Tell us about a lesson with which you were not satisfied. Why do you think that this lesson wasn't successful? What would you do the next time you taught it to improve the outcome of the lesson?

By becoming a reflective thinker, you are really forming your own philosophy of education. As you think about different aspects of your teaching paired with the different learning styles of students, you are raising your awareness of effective practices and developing your own style of teaching. You may be questioning some of the things you have learned and/or seen along the way as you develop your own set of teaching beliefs. In your reflection journal, note your thoughts. You may be asked to write about your own personal philosophy of education to be included in your professional portfolio. You may even be asked about it during an interview!

BEYOND THE MIRROR
As you learn and grow, use reflective thinking in other areas of your day as well. By asking yourself "I wonder" questions, you will understand more about people (students, colleagues, even family members) and make a positive difference in their lives.

The following scenario illustrates this idea:
After looking at your record book, you notice that Milo hasn't turned in his homework all week. As a consequence, you decide to have him miss recess and send him to study hall instead. The pattern continues until you start to think that Milo just does not care about his schoolwork and that he is not invested in his learning. Without reflective thinking, you might stop there and continue to send him to study hall day after day to help him "learn his lesson." A reflective teacher, however, would ask, "I wonder what is going on with Milo. He has turned in his homework all year, and now something has changed. What can I do to figure out what is going on with him?" You decide that you are going to speak with Milo privately to ask him why he has not been completing his homework recently. At first he says nothing and looks at the ground, but after further inquiry, Milo bursts into tears and tells you that he is being bullied out at

recess. He figured that the only way to escape the bullying was to not go to recess. He knew that if he didn't do his homework, he could stay in from recess and be safe. Imagine how you can now help Milo, and imagine what could have happened to Milo had you not taken the time to reflect upon the situation. In this case, reflective thinking on the teacher's part helped to discover a serious situation before it got worse.

Reflective thinking will improve your teaching in many ways. Take the time each day to think and reflect upon your instruction. Try not to dwell on what may have gone wrong. Instead, celebrate what went right! It is a good idea to keep a daily journal during your student teaching and into your first years in the classroom. It is quite rewarding to look back and see all that you have learned.

PASS THE ENVELOPE:
COMMUNICATING PROFESSIONALLY

You will need to professionally communicate in writing throughout your student teaching. With each document, you should consider many details: audience, form, tone, style, font, paper, etc. Included in this section are some writing samples to help guide your communication.

SAMPLE INTRODUCTION LETTER

Many times, your cooperating practitioner will write an introduction letter at the beginning of the school year and you should offer to do so as well. These letters set a positive tone right from the start!

Dear Families,

My name is Claudia Cole and I will be student teaching with Ms. Kurchian for the next 14 weeks. I am completing my senior year at Hope Valley University with a major in Elementary Education. Having met the 3rd graders, I already know that this is an extraordinary group of students who will teach me a great deal!

During my time at Forest Street Elementary School, I will have the opportunity to apply everything I've learned from my education. In addition, I know I will be learning so much more by working with Ms. Kurchian and your wonderful children so that I will be well-prepared for my goal - to help my students learn and grow as individuals.

Teaching is one of the most significant passions in my life and has been a career goal of mine since I was in elementary school myself. I feel that my love of children, education, and prior experience have prepared me for this final chapter in my education.

I am open to any questions, comments, or concerns that you may have and look forward to meeting each of you next week at Open House.

Cordially,

Ms. Claudia Cole

SAMPLE PHOTO/VIDEO/RESEARCH PERMISSION LETTER

If you will be taking photographs or video clips to use in your portfolio or for self-assessment, you will need to obtain parental permission. The following letter can be sent separately or be attached to your introduction letter. In this way, you will have plenty of time to obtain permission and will be able to start capturing on film your wonderful student teaching memories.

Parents/Guardians,

During my time in the classroom, I will be documenting my student teaching experience for my professional portfolio. With your permission, I would love to include photographs and video clips of the students and myself learning together (without using names) in my portfolio. In addition to developing my professional portfolio, I will be completing a research project on _____. As part of research, I may need to develop surveys or questionnaires and ask for you or your child to participate. This research will not be conducted until second semester once my teaching practicum is completed, which will require me to return to the classroom in the spring.

Please check below the appropriate statement, and return the slip to the classroom. Thank you in advance for fostering a positive learning experience for myself and the children.

Name of child: _____

_____ Yes, you have my permission to photograph/film lessons involving
        my child. No names will be attached.

_____ No, please do not photograph/film lessons involving my child.

_____ If the research topic is approved by the building principal and cooperating teacher,
        I give permission for my child to complete student surveys.

Parent/Guardian signature: _____

Date: _____

SAMPLE CLASSROOM VISITATION NOTE

Although you will be learning so much from observing and collaborating with your cooperating practitioner, there is a wealth of experience to be gained by observing other teachers "in action."

Toward the end of your student teaching, inquire about the possibility to observe other classrooms. It is interesting to see how other classrooms are physically set up, but even more valuable is observing the actions of the students as well as the teaching styles of other educators – varying grade levels, newer vs. veteran staff, special education, specialists (art, music, physical education, health, technology, etc.).

So as not to inconvenience anyone, obtain permission and set up appropriate times in advance by sending a friendly note to teachers in the building. And while visiting their classrooms, remember your observation skills from the beginning of your student teaching – again you are making a first impression on someone!

Dear Mrs. Giles,

I am currently student teaching in Ms. Audrey's classroom. Since I am seeking elementary certification, I feel it is important for me to observe both teachers and students in a variety of settings. I am interested in observing your classroom during the week of December 1st through 5th.

If it is possible for me to observe your classroom, please note below the day(s) and time(s) that work best for you and return this note to Ms. Audrey's mailbox. I look forward to a visit and thank you in advance for supporting an aspiring educator!

Sincerely,

Mr. Joel Tracy

SAMPLE GOOD-BYE LETTER

As much work as student teaching is, you will be amazed at how fast the time goes by. Toward the end of your practicum, sit back and reflect on how much you have learned from the students. Then take a moment to compose a thoughtful letter giving thanks to the parents and students for supporting your growth as an educator. You might even want to include a meaningful quote or special poem that represents your experience with the children.

Dear Families,

It is hard to believe that my time at Rock Point Academy is already coming to a close. The time has gone by too quickly! During my student teaching, everyone has been extremely supportive and made me feel so welcome. I am so fortunate to have had such an amazing experience.

The children have won a special place in my heart and have left a lasting impression on my life as an educator. They have taught me so much and helped me realize my potential as a teacher and what a unique profession I am entering. Each day was an adventure, and I will greatly miss, but surely never forget, their smiling faces!

At this time I would like to thank you for your generosity and kindness and your children for teaching me more than they'll ever know. I have been so fortunate to learn from Mrs. Milo as well. She has been a true mentor whose patience and guidance has inspired me. Each of you has played an important role in this wonderful experience that has impacted my life in such a positive way.

Once again, thank you for making my stay at Rock Point Academy so memorable. It has been a pleasure working in such a warm and caring environment.

Fondly,

Miss Ruby Janes

PUTTING IT ALL TOGETHER: ORGANIZING YOUR RESUME AND PROFESSIONAL PORTFOLIO

As your student teaching nears the end, get prepared to "sell" yourself, for you are about to enter the wonderful world of interviewing! Regardless of whether you are hand-delivering, mailing, or posting your information online, you will need three key documents to successfully prepare for the interview process: a cover letter, resume, and portfolio. A well-written cover letter and resume can land you that initial interview, and a professional portfolio can help seal the deal!

THE COVER LETTER
When you think about it, the interviewer actually "meets" your cover letter and resume before actually meeting you. So you want this first impression to be a good one. Since many people see the resume as "the main attraction," is a cover letter even necessary? The answer is simple: yes! A cover letter accompanies your resume to serve three purposes: introducing yourself, selling yourself, and encouraging further contact. It is a reflection of you that will either get your resume put aside into a pile or give it top priority. Aim for the top!

COVER LETTER HOW-TO
Find out the current contact person's name (and the correct spelling!), then address your cover letter accordingly. Most districts are now using an online applicant search site such as School Spring. Be sure to address your cover letter to the proper individual(s), especially if you are applying for multiple positions. If you are personally handing your resume to a principal, formally address your cover letter to that individual. If you are responding to an advertisement, use the information provided. If you are unable to find out the contact person's name, use "To whom it may concern." The salutation should lead the reader into three well-written paragraphs which are geared toward the particular position, school, or district to which you are applying. It may take more time to personalize each cover letter, but if it gets you in the door, it's worth it!

INTRODUCING . . . : THE WHO AND THE WHAT
In your first paragraph, briefly introduce yourself. Then clearly state the position in which you are interested and how you heard about the opening. If you are not responding to a particular job opening, identify the position(s) that interest you and for which you are certified, such as primary, intermediate, or middle school classroom teacher.

PICK ME! PICK ME!: THE WHY
Your second paragraph should highlight your key qualifications, specifically how your accomplishments, skills, and experience make you the perfect match for the position, school, district, etc. It is a sales pitch, so sell yourself! Note that you've enclosed your

resume, but DO NOT JUST REPEAT YOUR RESUME INFORMATION. Instead, this portion of the cover letter should whet the reader's appetite and serve as an invitation to turn the page!

SIGNING OFF: THE WHEN AND THE HOW
In your last paragraph, let the reader know you are thankful for his/her time and consideration. Open the door to further communication by identifying when and how you can be reached and that you look forward to a personal meeting. Include any pertinent contact information and respectfully sign off with "sincerely" and a neat, legible signature.

COVER LETTER DETAILS
Think of this letter as an "at-a-glance" advertisement of your personality, qualifications, and communication skills all at once. Your cover letter should be no longer than one page. Spark the reader's interest in you by stating information in an upbeat and positive manner using carefully chosen language. If your personality shines through in your cover letter, your resume will speak for itself!

SAMPLE COVER LETTER

Dear Mr. Connor,

It is with sincere interest that I am applying for the position of fifth grade teacher for the Redding Public School District recently posted in Redding News Today. I am a highly qualified candidate who is Massachusetts-certified with a Bachelor's degree in Elementary Education. In addition, I am enthusiastic and well-prepared to contribute my knowledge to your public school program, its curriculum and instruction, and its students' achievement and success.

As my enclosed resume indicates, I have lots to offer the Redding Public School District as an elementary classroom teacher. With experience as an innovative student teacher, using research-based teaching strategies, advanced technology, and current learning theories, setting high academic objectives as put forth in the Common Core and Massachusetts Curriculum Standards, and providing students with a safe, child-centered learning environment, I have a proven record for exceeding student teacher standards and demonstrating excellent interpersonal communication skills.

Please do not hesitate to contact me at (978) 555-1234 or at bjackson@aspiringteacher.net to set up a personal interview. Otherwise, I will call you next week to follow up on this application. I look forward to meeting with you to discuss how I can be an asset to the Redding Public School District. Thank you in advance for your time and consideration.

Sincerely,

Miss Brianna Jackson

THE RESUME

You have taken all the required courses and gained invaluable firsthand experience through student teaching. You're finally ready to teach! So it's time to create a professional resume to document all of these accomplishments in a way that will assist you in landing that first teaching position. Principals receive hundreds of professional resumes each year, and they typically give each one only a 20-second scan at first. How can you make yours stand out amongst the others?

RESUME HOW-TO

The first step to successful resume-writing is to reflect upon your experiences. Brainstorm your accomplishments as they apply to the field of education. (Remember that it does not have to be a paid position to count as experience!) Consider the following headings and examples to help you get your ideas on paper.

- FIELD EXPERIENCE: Student Teacher, Volunteer, Undergraduate Teaching Assistant
- PROFESSIONAL EXPERIENCE: Substitute Teacher, Day Care Provider, After-School Program Instructor, Coach, Summer Camp Counselor, Tutor
- LEADERSHIP OPPORTUNITIES: Peer Leader, Athletic Team Captain, Committee Chair

Once you have your initial ideas on paper, select the most relevant categories upon which to expand and combine or rearrange your experiences into these categories. For example, serving as an undergraduate teaching assistant can be considered a leadership role or professional experience. Choose accomplishments that you can describe in greater detail and that you will be able to discuss confidently during interviews. Each position should then be expanded to include at least three bulleted details that are written as sentence fragments that begin with various action verbs. Be consistent with the verb tense (i.e. with past experiences use past tense, with current experiences use present tense). Stick to the basic facts of the assignment, then include extra responsibilities and skills that transfer to the education field. In addition, try to use some of today's educational "buzzwords" when applicable.

FIELD EXPERIENCE EXAMPLE

Student Teacher, Sunshine Elementary School, Ridgeway, Massachusetts   Fall 2012
- Managed diverse needs of a third grade self-contained heterogeneous classroom of twenty regular and special education students
- Implemented state frameworks via district-wide curriculum and original lesson plans incorporating interactive technology
- Collaborated with classroom and special education teachers to modify instruction according to IEPs and other educational plans
- Communicated with parents via newsletters, conferences, and email
- Participated in report card conferences, professional development, staff meetings, and field trips

PROFESSIONAL EXPERIENCE EXAMPLE

Camp Counselor, All-Natural Summer Camp, Hillview, New Hampshire   2009-Present
- Supervise groups of six children ages 6-12
- Create and teach enrichment lessons centered on nature-based science themes such as ocean life, water pollution, and food chains
- Support professional staff in planning related field trips

LEADERSHIP OPPORTUNITIES EXAMPLE

Peer Leader, Endicott College, Beverly, Massachusetts   2009-2011
- Developed multi-media presentation for First Annual Pre-Student Teaching Workshop for incoming seniors with an education major
- Tutored peers in algebra and calculus in the Student Services Center
- Spoke on behalf of the Class of 2009 at the spring education banquet honoring cooperating practitioners and college supervisors

Additional categories may only require listed experiences instead of detailed descriptions. For instance, consider the following headings and examples.

- PROFESSIONAL DEVELOPMENT: *Differentiated Instruction in Science, Technology in the Classroom* (seminars/pre-service workshops)
- HONORS/AWARDS: Kappa Delta Pi Education Honor Society, Dean's List
- TECHNOLOGY SKILLS: Interactive Whiteboard (Smart Board), iPads and mobile devices, Presentation Software (Power Point)
- ADDITIONAL LANGUAGES: American Sign, Spanish, French
- PROFESSIONAL AFFILIATIONS: Association of Teachers of Mathematics in Massachusetts (ATMIM)
- CURRICULUM PROGRAMS AND PRACTICES: Everyday Mathematics, Guided Reading
- COLLEGE ACTIVITIES: Softball, Chorus, Chess Club

RESUME DETAILS

Now you're ready to put it all together. No matter what format you choose, you want your resume to be well-organized and concise. Consider this order of categories to start: heading, objective, education, and certification(s).

- Heading: Clearly list your name, address, telephone number, and email address; include both permanent and temporary contact information if applicable
- Objective: Briefly identify the grade level(s) and content area(s) in which you are interested and certified
- Education: Include any graduate and/or undergraduate degrees, institutions, and dates
- Certification: Specify all certifications, including subject areas, that you currently hold and/or that are pending: include certification numbers when applicable.

Next, prioritize and clearly label the remaining categories (brainstormed above in the HOW-TO section) in order of importance. Under each heading, be sure to list your experiences with the most current being first. Include the more detailed headings first, followed by the listed experiences. Lastly, state that references are available upon request (and be sure you actually have them available!).

Overall, your resume should be appealing, easy-to-read, and no more than 1 or 2 pages in length. Your resume is another representation of how effectively you can communicate. Therefore, make sure it is your best work. Don't forget to check (and double-check) your spelling and grammar before neatly sending it off with your cover letter and any other requested materials (transcripts, letters of recommendation, etc.) in a full-sized envelope. In the end, remember that a superior resume can be modern and eye-catching, yet still maintain an air of professionalism and confidence. Once you look at your completed resume, you will proudly pat yourself on the back for yet another job well done!

NAYA JANE D'ANNA

716 Barrows Avenue, Red Corner City, MA 54321

(781) 555-1234   ndanna@aspiringteacher.net

Energetic, resourceful, dedicated teacher with the ability to:
- develop, implement, and collect data on standards-based curriculum
- effectively collaborate with the school community
- foster and support an inclusion-based learning environment and curriculum
- use innovative technology to enhance student learning

CERTIFICATION

Massachusetts Initial Certification
#123456789

Early Childhood Certification (Pre-K-2)
Special Education Certification (N-9)

EDUCATION

Ipswich River University, Stonington, MA
Bachelor of Arts: Early Childhood Education
Major GPA: 3.9

May, 2010

FIELD EXPERIENCE

Student Teacher: K/ 1 Inclusion Classroom
Woodside Elementary School, Macy Gap, MA

Fall, 2009

- Designed standards-based units, curriculum, and assessments
- Incorporated the Multiple Intelligence Theory and differentiated instruction into teaching
- Developed various behavior modification programs
- Communicated with parents via home-school journals, newsletters, emails, and meetings
- Participated on the Teacher Assistance Team, attended PTO events, staff meetings, and professional development opportunities

---

PROFESSIONAL EXPERIENCE

Educational Assistant: Autism Spectrum Program
Woodside Elementary School, Macy Gap, MA

Spring, 2009

- Assisted in developing, writing, implementing, and collecting data for IEPs
- Attended weekly meetings to support special education students
- Supported classroom teachers to best include students on the spectrum within the classrooms
- Communicated daily with parents via home/school journals, Email, phone, and/or notices
- Used assistive technology to enhance/support students' learning

---

CURRICULUM PROGRAMS

Everyday Mathematics	Fundations Phonics	John Collins Writing
Science and Technology for Children	CAFÉ/Daily 5	Junior Great Books

---

REFERENCES: Available upon request

THE PORTFOLIO

Your professional portfolio is a tangible representation of your educational achievements. By gathering evidence of your accomplishments into one place, you will have an invaluable tool to use during the interview process and as a future reference once you've started your career.

PORTFOLIO HOW-TO

Since the end of your student teaching can be an especially hectic time, start collecting portfolio contents early. You will be thankful you did! What do you include? If your college has specific portfolio requirements, use those guidelines. Otherwise, consider including the following items.

- Table of contents
- Cover letter
- Resume
- Philosophy of education
- Supervisor's evaluations
- Letters of recommendation
- Personal reflections
- List of references
- Official college transcripts
- Certification
- Sample lesson plans (including original activity pages, assessment, etc.)
- Student samples (names removed)
- Incentive/classroom management program description
- Photographs (of you teaching, students learning, products, performances, displays, etc.)
- Student evaluations
- Positive notes from parents or students (names removed)

PORTFOLIO DETAILS

While your cover letter and resume are formal documents, your professional portfolio can show off more of your personality and creativity if you choose. You can use a colorful binder, printed stationery, sheet protectors, etc. to spice it up. Here is yet another place to utilize technology. Done well, electronic portfolios and photo books are quite impressive. Perhaps you'd like to add inspirational quotes or poetry. However creative you choose to get with your portfolio, be sure you know the contents inside and out so that you can use it strategically and efficiently to enhance your interview experience. Consider organizing the materials by state standards and/or use labeled dividers to tab your sections for easy reference. That way you are showing off your organizational skills as well as selling yourself!

HELP WANTED: STAMPS OF APPROVAL
OBTAINING YOUR LETTERS OF RECOMMENDATION

Although documents such as your cover letter, resume, and portfolio speak volumes about you, administrators also rely quite heavily on letters of recommendation as they provide another assessment of your student teaching performance and your potential as an educator.

What is typically included in a letter of recommendation?
Although letters of recommendation are usually only about one page in length, they can provide a wealth of information about your accomplishments during student teaching and/or your potential as an aspiring educator.

The basics of a letter of recommendation include descriptions of your:
- Student teaching placement: name, type, and size of school, the length of your practicum, subjects and/or grades taught, number of students, type of classroom (inclusion, self-contained, mixed-grade)
- Teaching responsibilities and abilities: specific lessons/units taught, type of instruction (small group, whole class, one-to-one, co-teaching), special projects, assessment experience
- Academic background: relevant coursework, understanding of educational theories and best practices
- Extra-curricular and/or volunteer activities
- Education-related qualities: professionalism, dedication, maturity, organization, communication skills
- Special talents displayed during student teaching such as technology expertise, musical ability, etc.
- Overall potential as an educator in a final statement

Who should I ask for a letter of recommendation?
Letters of recommendation should be written by individuals who have knowledge of your academic experience, your career goals, and your overall teaching ability and potential. The two most important sources for letters of recommendation are your COOPERATING PRACTIONER and your COLLEGE SUPERVISOR. These are the two people who have had the chance to work closely with you and to observe your growth throughout your student teaching.

Others you may consider asking include:
- Professors of education courses or on-campus advisors (who can speak of your leadership qualities, work ethic, and academic performance)

- School principal or other administrators (if a positive relationship has been formed and he/she has observed you teaching a lesson)
- Other professionals with whom you may have closely collaborated during student teaching (special educator, reading specialist, etc.)
- Supervisors of education-related experience (substitute teaching, camp counseling, etc.)
- Parent (if a relationship has developed during the semester)
- You may even include a student letter as an extra – after all, children always speak the truth!

Plan to obtain between 3-5 letters of recommendation in all. Since some individuals may feel uncomfortable writing formal letters, be sure to ask others as back up if you note any hesitation at all.

How and when should I ask for letters of recommendation?

Since a letter of recommendation is a reflection of you, you should ask for one politely and in person. You can always follow up with a reminder note. As you may be asked, be willing and prepared to include a list of your major accomplishments or even a copy of your resume.

You should ask for letters of recommendation AT LEAST TWO WEEKS before your student teaching ends. If you are asking individuals on your college campus (professors, college activity advisors, etc.), be sure to ask in advance and obtain the letters before the end of the semester. This will give most people ample time. However, in some instances, individuals may be more comfortable handing you a letter AFTER the completion of your practicum. Be patient and appreciative – a favorable and well-written letter of recommendation should be considered a gift. And as with any gift, be sure to follow up with a handwritten thank you note to show your gratitude!

NOTE: Upon receiving your letters of recommendation, be sure they are signed by the writer. Then make numerous copies as you will need to include them in your portfolio as well as with most of the applications you submit.

What is the difference between a recommendation and a reference?

Letters of recommendation are formal documents which should be included in your portfolio and with most of the applications you submit. References are individuals who are willing to speak on your behalf in an informal setting, such as a telephone conference or by email. It is common to have the same individuals who wrote you letters listed as references as well.

Your reference page should include the names, positions, institution/company/district, addresses, phone numbers, and email addresses of the individuals who have given you explicit permission to list them. Again, a sincere thank you goes a long way when you've been given a "stamp of approval"!

HELP WANTED: ON THE SPOT
PREPARING FOR (AND NAILING) YOUR INTERVIEWS

BEFORE THE BIG DAY:

In reality, your initial interview with an administrator begins when you answer your telephone to arrange for your first meeting, so remember to speak with confidence and maturity. Do your best to accommodate the times which are available. Remember this could be your future principal!

Should I attend job fairs?

ABSOLUTELY! Attending job fairs is one of the best ways to help you prepare for an interview. You want to make sure that you visit many different school district tables and speak with as many different educators or administrators as you can. Save a few top picks for last, that way you will have had plenty of experience before you meet with the districts with which you hope to have an interview.

Should I research the school in advance?

Do your homework. Learn as much as you can about the school and district in which you will be interviewing.   Reading local newspapers will give you background information about a community's school system. Check out the district's website to read the profile about each school and its staff.   For example, if you are interviewing for a third-grade position, try to find out the names of the third-grade teachers, the projected class size, and the curriculum currently being used. If this information is not available, formulate questions to ask later in the interview.

We recommend that you also Mapquest, Google, or GPS directions and do a practice drive to the school. This way, on the day of your interview you will not have to think about getting lost, finding out where to park your car, etc. You will have enough on your mind!

What should I bring?

Get organized in advance. Make extra packets of your interview materials (your cover letter, resume, letters of recommendation, transcripts, etc.). Also pack your professional portfolio.

How will I use my professional portfolio?

Be sure you are very familiar with the components of your portfolio. Remember, the ONLY work that should be included in your portfolio is work that YOU created or work that you had a hand in creating. In advance of an interview, mark off your favorite lesson or other examples of work that you would like to showcase during your interview. Since your interview may only be about 30 minutes long, you should plan on sharing your portfolio work while answering questions. For example, if you are asked to share your literacy experiences with the interview team, you should answer the question AND share something from your portfolio that shows evidence of your response. Unfortunately, if you don't use your portfolio in this interactive manner, in many cases interviewers will only give your portfolio a "courtesy glance" at the end of your interview. Remember the old saying: a picture is worth a thousand words!

HOT TIP: As crazy as this may sound, practice your "interviewing" skills any time you can – like whenever you're driving, looking in the mirror, into a tape or video recorder, or with a friend! Ask yourself questions ALOUD, and then answer the questions ALOUD. This truly will help you. You will catch yourself on some occasions starting to ramble on and on. That's your cue that you need to refine your responses. The more you hear yourself speak, the less likely you are to use slang (you guys, I'm gonna, like, wicked, ummm, you know, etc.), and the more comfortable you will become for the big interview.

THE BIG DAY:

On the big day, be sure to eat a healthy breakfast or lunch to give yourself the extra energy that you will need. The hours before your interview may feel more like days! Do your best to relax; if you have followed the above suggestions, then you are prepared.

What should I wear?

The most important piece of advice we can offer is to look professional. This doesn't mean you need to go out and purchase a new suit, but do your best to put together a conservative outfit that fits you well. Now that you're dressed and ready, grab those interview materials and off you go!

What should I expect when I arrive at the school?

Politely identify yourself as soon as you enter the building as most schools have a security policy. Unless you are told otherwise, report to the main office. There you will most likely be greeted by the school receptionist. Be pleasant and friendly; the school secretary is often the principal's right hand person! Once you have introduced yourself, you will be asked to sit and wait until you are called in to meet with the principal or team. When you are called, be sure to stand tall, be confident, and enter with a smile. As you introduce yourself again, offer your hand and give a firm handshake. Wait until you are asked to be seated before doing so. (Remember YOU ONLY GET ONE CHANCE!)

Who could be at my interview, and what will I be asked?

An interview may be with a committee of as many as 5+ people. Interview panel members may include the principal, assistant principal, teachers on the grade-level team with which you would be working, reading specialist, special education teacher, parent(s) and/or school counselor. Usually one member of the committee at a time will ask a question. Listen carefully to each question. Ask for clarification if necessary. Think about your honest answer. Look your interviewer in the eye, and do your best to restate the question as part of your opener. Give specific examples to substantiate your response, and use your portfolio!

Here are some sample interview questions that candidates may be asked during a first interview. So, let's answer some questions!

QUESTIONS ABOUT YOURSELF

- Tell us something about yourself that we may not know from your resume.
- What special talents or expertise could you bring to our school district?
- We have read your application and resume, but what are the most important things we should know about you?
- Who has most influenced you to become an educator? How?
- What would your previous employer, college advisor, or cooperating teacher say were your greatest teaching strengths, and what areas would he/she suggest were areas that need growth?
- What are you a "6" at now, but wish to be a "10"?
- If your greatest supporter was in the room with us today, what five words would he/she use to describe you as a person? A teacher? A colleague?
- Why did you choose teaching as a career?
- What would you never want to do as a teacher and why?
- Give an example of a time you went "above and beyond."

- Are you a risk taker? Explain.
- What do you think is the difference between a good teacher and a great teacher?

QUESTIONS ABOUT STUDENTS

- Tell me about a difficult circumstance you have handled. What action did you take? What were the results?
- What is your approach to classroom management and student discipline?
- What would you do to develop a good teacher-student relationship?
- A student in your class consistently causes disruptions. Explain the steps you would take to remedy the situation and your reasoning for each step.
- How would you ensure that your classroom is an exciting place - a place where students are always engaged?
- What would your classroom look like: the physical set-up AND the students learning in it?
- How have you used or would you use technology to involve students in their own learning?

QUESTIONS ABOUT CURRICULUM, INSTRUCTION, AND ASSESSMENT

- Describe your student teaching experience.
- What was the most rewarding/frustrating/surprising thing that happened during your student teaching?
- How would you incorporate the learning styles of individuals into your teaching?
- What strategies would you use to help prepare students for meeting grade-level standards?
- How would you use data to improve classroom instruction?
- What content area do you see as your strength? Your weakness?
- If I were to visit your classroom and take a photo, what would I see in that photo?
- What have you read lately that led you to change the way you teach?
- What's new in education about which you would like to learn more?
- Explain in 100 words or less your philosophy of teaching.
- What methods of teaching, besides lecture, would you use to present material to your students?
- Describe a lesson that you have taught that you feel went very well. Explain why you feel that this was a good lesson.
- Share something you learned from a lesson that didn't go so well.
- What if your students don't "get it"? In other words, if a lesson is not working for all your students, what is your plan for remediation? How would you implement that plan?
- What type(s) of technology have you effectively used in your lessons?

QUESTIONS ABOUT SCHOOL, COMMUNITY, AND PARENTS

- How important is collaboration and building camaraderie with other staff members? How would you go about this?
- We are working hard to turn our school into a "learning community." What special skills, talents, or knowledge will you bring to this community?
- Explain what professionalism means to you within the school climate and outside the school.
- In what ways do you involve parents in the learning process or in classroom activities?
- Imagine that you have been hired as the newest member of our teaching team. In less than three minutes, how would you introduce yourself to a group of parents, students, and teachers of our school?
- How would you communicate to a parent how a student is performing academically and/or socially?
- Our district offers many opportunities for professional development. What type of professional development interests you, and how would you take advantage of such an environment? To what professional development area(s) do you see yourself contributing in the future?
- How will you enhance our goal of being an effective learning-focused school as opposed to a teaching-focused school?
- What are the expectations you hold for your principal?

WRITE NOW!

Sometimes candidates are asked to answer a question or respond to a prompt in writing before, during, or after an interview. The interviewer may want to judge your communication skills, so practice how you'd communicate effectively and professionally with parents, students, or colleagues. (Brush up on capitalization, grammar, punctuation, and spelling as well!)

How will my interview end?

An interview will usually end with the big question: What questions do YOU have for us? Consider asking:

- What type of professional development is offered?
- Will there be opportunities to work with colleagues on district-wide or school-based committees?
- Describe the culture of the school.
- Is there a mentor program in place? How does it work?
- What are the projected or average class sizes at the school?
- Tell me about your most updated technology.
- Describe the team with which I'd be working.
- What are the next steps of the interview process?

Although you will still be nervous, end your interview as professionally as it began. Look the interviewers in the eye, shake their hands again, thank them for their time, and comment, "It was very nice meeting everyone. I look forward to hearing from you soon."

THANKS A BUNCH!
After your interview, follow-up with a thank you note to the principal or lead interviewer. A thank you note shows both professionalism and polite manners. It will also make you stand out. Within 24 hours, send a brief, hand-written note stating your appreciation for the interview, a positive comment about the staff, school, or district, and your continued interest in the position. A thank you note will leave yet another positive impression of you.

Remember, whether you get the position or not, each interview should be seen as a learning experience. With each one, you will build more confidence and boost your interviewing skills until the right position for you comes along.

DEAR ABBY:
QUESTIONS FREQUENTLY ASKED DURING STUDENT TEACHING

It is inevitable that questions will arise during your student teaching that may not be addressed in this guide. However, the following represents some of the questions most frequently asked during this important stage in your career. Whatever your question(s) may be, be sure to maintain your professionalism and remain confidential as you seek out the person most likely to be of assistance. Listen openly to any advice offered.

- Dear Abby,
  I feel as if I am ready to take on more teaching responsibility, but my cooperating teacher only allows me to do "busy work" like correcting and filing papers and walking the students to and from specialists (art, physical education, music, etc.). What should I do?

  Dear Student Teacher,
  It is great that you feel you are ready to take on more responsibility. Way to be a go-getter! The best advice is to be honest and upfront with your cooperating teacher. We suggest that you ask to meet with your cooperating teacher during a prep time or before/after school. During this time, you can let your cooperating teacher know how you feel and that you think you are ready to take on more of a teaching role. It may be helpful to share your semester guidelines with your cooperating teacher and try to map out a take-over plan. If for any reason after speaking with your cooperating teacher you are not assigned further teaching responsibility within the next week, be sure to speak with your supervisor about the situation.

- Dear Abby,
  Sometimes I feel that my cooperating teacher is placing too much responsibility on me. I have so much of my own coursework to do that I feel overwhelmed. How can I manage it all?

  Dear Student Teacher,
  Welcome to the world of teaching! One of the greatest challenges of teaching is trying to balance all that is needed to do and still manage to sleep and eat, too! Your cooperating teacher must feel that you are ready to take on more of a responsibility. That's a compliment to you! Take your student teaching placement seriously, and do your best to budget your time. Remember, this could be or lead to your future workplace, if you prove yourself. Yes, it is true, you'll be spending many nights lesson plan writing and prepping the seemingly endless supply of materials you will need to carry out these lessons while your friends are hitting the town. Nevertheless, remember that it is all worth it in the end.

- Dear Abby,

  It seems as if the theories I learned in my coursework are not reflected in the practices I see in my placement. Is there anything I can do?

  Dear Student Teacher,
  There is nothing better than seeing firsthand the theories you learned about in your coursework being put into action in the classroom. It makes your learning come alive! However, this is not always the case. Sometimes school districts and/or classroom teachers are not on the cutting edge of current practices. Although teachers may be aware of these new current practices, they may choose not to implement them because it means change. Whatever the case may be, you want to do your best to make the most of your practicum. Try to make connections with what you have learned in class to what you are seeing in the classroom. Ask questions. You can tell your cooperating teacher what you are learning and ask him/her about his/her views on the topic. You may even end up teaching your cooperating practitioner something! If you feel that you have been placed in a classroom where you are not being provided with a meaningful learning experience, be sure to speak with your supervisor as soon as you can. Do not wait until your first observation to bring this up. Time is of the essence!

- Dear Abby,

  Help! The students listen to me so well when my cooperating practitioner is in the classroom. However, as soon as she leaves chaos ensues! All of a sudden, they start chatting with their friends and "goofing around." Do you have any suggestions to help them see me as their teacher whether or not my cooperating practitioner is in the room?

  Dear Student Teacher,
  It would not be a true learning experience if your students did not do this to you at first! They are trying to figure out just how much they can push. If you do not nip it in the bud, you will never earn their respect. Right from the start, closely observe your cooperating teacher when he/she is teaching to notice all the subtle and silent cues that he/she does without missing a beat in the instruction. Then try holding a brief class meeting with your students before your first take-over lesson. Let it be known that when you are teaching, you are also in charge and will hold them to the same expectations to which their classroom teacher holds them. Also think about initiating a classroom incentive plan. Developing a positive and effective classroom management plan is truly one of the greatest challenges you will face, not only during your practicum, but also well into your first years as a teacher.

- Dear Abby,
  During take-over week, is it appropriate to teach with my own style although it may be quite different from my cooperating teacher's?

  Dear Student Teacher,
  One of the greatest aspects of teaching is that you can let your own unique personality shine through! Your personality shapes your teaching style. You want to be sure, however, that you respect the culture and climate that has been established within the classroom by your cooperating teacher. If you are in a great placement, then you will learn so many wonderful things from your cooperating teacher, one of which is how to develop your own teaching style. The importance of open communication and honesty cannot be stressed enough. Talk with your cooperating teacher about his/her style, how it came to be, and if it has changed over the years. You may learn a lot from this one conversation alone.

- Dear Abby,
  What can I do to "fit in" right from the start of school?

  Dear Student Teacher,
  The best way to "fit in" is to "get in there" and join the classroom community. Do not sit at the back table and write things in a notebook. ACTIVELY OBSERVE! Greet the students as they enter the classroom and engage in a conversation with a few of them as they get themselves settled. Be sure to walk around the classroom, there is ALWAYS someone that needs some kind of help. If your cooperating teacher starts passing out papers, take a stack and help. Ask the cooperating teacher how you can best assist. In short, make the most of your experience!

- Dear Abby,
  I just taught a lesson that completely flopped! What should I do?

  Dear Student Teacher,
  Celebrate that the lesson is over ... and do not worry; it happens to the best of us! What is most important, and what separates the good from the exemplary teacher is what you do AFTER the lesson. Take some time and look over your lesson plan. Think about the point during the lesson when things started to go downhill. Ask yourself why this happened. Ask your cooperating teacher to reflect with you. Once you have identified what went wrong, think about what you could have done or what you will do the next time you teach the lesson. If you look at every lesson that flops as a learning experience, you will grow into a reflective and proactive teacher.

Dear Abby,

I took a great course on technology and I would LOVE to integrate some web 2.0 things into my lessons. The problem is my cooperating teacher is just learning how to use her new interactive white board. What should I do?

Dear Student Teacher,

Technology, in all forms, can be very intimidating for many teachers, especially for those who have not had proper training and professional development. Why not suggesting that the two of you meet one day after school so that you can switch roles-you can be the teacher and your cooperating practitioner can be your student! You can start the conversation by letting him/her know about the course you took and some of the neat things that you learned. You can ask if you can use some of the technology ideas in your upcoming lessons.

WHAT'S ALL THE BUZZ?
STUDENT TEACHING A-Z:
DEFINING KEY EDUCATIONAL TERMS

Education is an ever-changing field, vocabulary included. Therefore it is important to familiarize yourself with the current educational jargon and "buzzwords." Since you will be hearing these key educational terms during your own education, within your student teaching practicum, while interviewing, and into your educational career, you will want to understand and properly apply these terms. Take the time to research the following list of terms that includes some of today's educational buzzwords.

- 21st Century skills and Learning

- accommodations

- accuracy

- activation of prior knowledge

- adequate yearly progress

- algorithm

- alignment

- alternative assessment

- assessment

- at-risk students

- authentic assessment (formative/summative)

- benchmarks

- blog

- Bloom's taxonomy

- brainstorming

- BYOD

- CAFÉ/Daily 5

- certificated

- collaborative/cooperative learning

- common core standards

- comprehension

- concept mapping

- constructivism

- cooperating practitioner

- curriculum mapping

- data collection

- differentiated instruction

- expository writing

- flipped classrooms

- fluency

- Fundations

- guided reading

- guiding principles

- highly qualified teacher

- inclusion

- Individualized Education Plan (IEP)

- inquiry-based learning

- learning centers

- learning outcomes

- learning styles

- literacy

- manipulatives

- metacognition

- narrative writing

- No Child Left Behind Act (NCLB)

- performance assessment

- persuasive writing

- phonemic awareness

- phonics

- portfolio

- prior knowledge

- professional development

- proficiency

- resource teacher

- rubric

- RTI

- scaffolded instruction

- School Improvement Plan (SIP)

- self-assessment

- SMART goals

- special education

- staff development days

- standards-based education

- student teacher

- supervisor

- teacher evaluation process

- tiered instruction model (TIM)

- vocabulary

- wiki

Q-AND-A: GUIDED READING IN THE CLASSROOM

If you haven't learned about guided reading in your courses or pre-practicum, you should become familiar with the term: what it means, how it is used in the classroom, the reasoning behind this instructional reading approach, and most importantly, how it is implemented in today's classrooms. The term "guided reading" was originally coined in the late nineties by reading teachers and researchers Irene Fountas and Gay Su Pinnell when they published their book Guided Reading: Good First Teaching for All Children. (This book would be a great resource in which to invest!) For now, it is imperative that you at least have the basics of guided reading.

WHAT IS GUIDED READING?

Guided reading is an instructional reading approach designed to help individual students learn how to decode, comprehend, and fluently read a variety of increasingly challenging books of all genres with direct and proper support and scaffolding from a teacher. In guided reading, the teacher brings together, and therefore focuses instruction on, groups of students who are similar in their reading needs and strengths.

WHAT IS THE RATIONALE?

The basic rationale behind guided reading is that all students need ongoing reading instruction throughout their elementary and middle school years, regardless of the "grade level" at which they can read. At first, the purpose of guided reading is to support students as they "learn to read," while during their upper elementary years, the purpose of guided reading shifts to help those same students develop strategies to help them "read to learn." Within the guided reading setting, the goal is to expand students' abilities to use background knowledge, decode words, check on their reading, access and use information, think beyond the text, connect the text to self, world, and other texts, develop fluent reading behaviors, and think about the text critically.

During guided reading, teachers have the opportunity to better learn about the individual students as readers due to the small-group setting. Anecdotal records, observation, and informal assessment based on guided reading assignments, reading ability, and participation provide valuable assessment. Teachers should develop their own personal record-keeping system to match their needs.

HOW ARE THE STUDENTS GROUPED?

The goal of guided reading is to form small groups of students who are similar in their reading developmental level and read approximately the same level of text. Ideally, guided reading groups are *flexible* as students' needs and/or lesson goals change.

There are many formal tests available to help group students according to their needs. Some include: Gaites MacGinitie, Developmental Reading Assessment, Scholastic Reading Inventory, etc. Informal assessment, record-keeping, and observation are extremely valuable as well.

HOW ARE TEXTS SELECTED?

Generally, texts are chosen based on their text difficulty/readability level. Fountas and Pinnell used a specific formula to determine the readability level of specific books, but now, since the practice of guided reading is so commonly used in classrooms, many publishers print the "level" of their books right on the cover, which makes it even easier for teachers to match books to their students. In addition, leveled texts can also be chosen by genre, theme, subject or author, depending on the teacher's lesson goals. Alternating longer with shorter texts and fiction with non-fiction texts provides more opportunity for flexibility amongst groups.

WHAT SPACE AND MATERIALS ARE NEEDED?

Minimal space and a selection of texts are necessary to initiate guided reading. More materials and texts can be added as needed. A round table works well so that all the readers can see and hear each other which will further facilitate the conversation and focus the lesson. Other materials useful during guided reading may include: highlighters, highlighting tape, sticky notes, writing utensils, white boards, easel, and/or teacher resources.

HOW DO YOU SCHEDULE GUIDED READING?

Explicit instruction of strategies is essential and makes reading more powerful for all students. Teachers should adopt a schedule that allows some time for whole-class opening (and later closing) of skill instruction, but allocates most time to instructional time with guided reading. Since guided reading is considered the most important part of a balanced literacy program, it is good practice for there to be some form of a guided reading block every day.

In a typical primary classroom, three 20-minute guided reading groups can meet daily with the teacher. Depending on the number of groups, each group meets at least twice weekly with the teacher. (It is recommended that struggling readers meet with the teacher at least 4 times a week.) The remaining students are working in small groups actively engaged in various "literacy center" activities. These centers are often theme- or content area-based and include a variety of language arts activities related to reading, writing, spelling, phonics, comprehension, and listening. The classroom teacher determines the literacy centers.*

In a typical intermediate classroom, four guided reading groups can each meet with the teacher twice weekly for 20-30 minutes each meeting. The remaining students work independently on "menu items" that provide meaningful language arts experiences including reading, writing, spelling, vocabulary, grammar, guided reading skill assignments, etc. This menu is determined by the classroom teacher.*

*After introducing a key strategy whole-class, the teacher should integrate it into meaningful literacy centers and/or menu activities the students can work on independently or in small groups. (The same key strategy is the focus of guided reading instruction as well.) Students can later be assessed on this skill.

WHAT IS THE TEACHER'S ROLE DURING GUIDED READING?

Although students are reading the same text, they all read silently at their own pace. The teacher asks individual students to slightly "turn up their voices" and read a portion of the selection aloud. While listening to each student, the teacher notes specific reading behaviors. Therefore, the teacher does spend some time listening to individual students read aloud; however, discussing and revisiting the text are often the focus of time spent with the groups. The activities that follow reading draw attention back to the text and build on the learning that took place earlier in the lesson.

The teacher should...
•highlight one or two important skills/strategies
•discuss the application of the skills/strategy
•talk with students about the meaning of the text
•enrich vocabulary by highlighting some words from the text
•have students go on a "picture walk" if appropriate to preview and predict

...and invite them to...
•make connections
•revisit the text to search for more information
•find evidence to support their thinking
•clarify meaning
•search for themes
•notice the author's use of language
•provide evidence from the text to back up their conclusions about a book

WHAT IS THE STUDENTS' ROLE DURING GUIDED READING?
Following the introduction, each student silently reads the entire text or a unified portion of it. Guided reading differs from traditional group instruction in which "round robin reading" - students taking turns reading aloud - holds center stage. In guided reading, students are expected to embrace the role of reader independently.

The students should...
•silently read
•actively use processing strategies to solve problems while reading
•anticipate discussion and accordingly focus on particular aspects of the text
•use sticky notes to provide evidence and/or identify and remember questions

IS GUIDED READING THE BE-ALL END-ALL?

Not at all! Remember, as critical as guided reading (instructional level text) is, it is just one part of a balanced reading program. Other components include: independent reading (fluent level text), partner or whole-class shared reading (grade-level text), and reading aloud to the students (advanced level text).

RESOURCES:

Fountas, Irene C. and Gay Su Pinnell. **Guided Reading: Good First Teaching for All Students.** Portsmouth: Heinemann, 1996.

Fountas, Irene C. and Gay Su Pinnell. **Guiding Readers and Writers Grades 3-6: Teaching Comprehension, Genre, and Content Literacy**. Portsmouth: Heinemann, 2001.